THE LOW DOWN

*A Guide to Creating
Supportive Jazz Bass Lines*

by

Danny Ziemann

© 2015 Danny Ziemann

©2015 Danny Ziemann

Published by the Institute for Creative Music, Inc.

All Rights Reserved.
No part of this publication may be reproduced,
stored in retrieval system, or transmitted, in any form or by any means,
electronic, mechanical, photocopying, recording or otherwise,
without prior written permission from Institute for Creative Music
www.ifcmusic.org

ISBN-13: 978-0692405956 (Institute for Creative Music, Inc.)
ISBN-10: 069240595X

Cover Design: Dave Chisholm
Book Formatting: Keenan Bartlett
Cover Formatting: Matthew Golombisky
Editing: Kim Teal and Chris Teal
Biography Photo: Aaron Winters
Back Cover Photo: Nadine Sherman

Recordings Tracked by: John Nyerges and Gabriel Flores
Recordings Mixed and Mastered by: John Nyerges

Personnel:
Piano - John Nyerges
Drums - Chris Teal

Examples were recorded with a Neumann TLM103, 1 foot in front of the F Hole (treble side). Danny plays a Shen SB300 with D'Addario Pizzicato (HB610) strings.

Supplemental recordings for this book are available for download at www.DannyZiemann.com

Acknowledgments

This book would not have been possible without the support of the following people:

My family and close loved ones,

Chris Teal, Kim Teal, and the IFCM for investing so much energy into this book,

Keenan Bartlett, Dave Chisholm, and Matthew Golombisky for your design talents,

Jeff Campbell, James VanDemark, Wayne Moose, and Bill Dobbins for invaluable musical instruction and guidance,

Larry Grenadier for your mentorship and contributions to this book,

John Nyerges for your recording and musical contributions,

John Fetter and Chris Azzara for your educational guidance,

Howard Potter and the Eastman Community Music School for their generous financial support,

Lyris Hung and the folks at D'Addario for their extreme generosity.

To all who contributed and played a part in this, thank you!

About the Author

Danny Ziemann is a jazz bassist, educator, and composer living in Rochester, NY. A 2012 graduate of the Eastman School of Music with degrees in Music Education and Jazz Bass Performance, he has been freelancing since the age of 16: currently throughout New York State and additionally tours internationally with band leader Gordon Webster. He can be seen performing at the Xerox Rochester International Jazz Festival, and venues in Rochester and Buffalo, sharing the stage with greats including Bill Dobbins, Don Menza, Delfeayo Marsalis, Gene Bertoncini, Dennis Mackrel, and Bobby Militello. Danny's teachers include Jeff Campbell, James VanDemark and Bill Dobbins.

As the Instructor of Jazz Bass at the Eastman Community Music School and at SUNY Oswego, Danny balances performing with a full teaching schedule. Danny is also a Teaching Artist for the Institute for Creative Music, holds his New York State Teacher Certification, is an active guest clinician and teacher at college-based music camps during the Summer, and is a contributing writer to D'Addario's newest blog *Behind the Bridge*. Education and the learning process is extremely important to Danny, and he strives to advance jazz bass pedagogy.

For updates on Danny's performance and teaching schedule, visit www.DannyZiemann.com

Table of Contents

Foreword..6

Preface...7

Chapter 1: The Warm-Up...9

Chapter 2: Developing a Layout of Your Instrument..14

Chapter 3: Fundamental Bass line Construction..22

Chapter 4: Rhythm Changes..38

Chapter 5: Modal Tunes...46

Chapter 6: Advanced Line Construction...51

Chapter 7: The Two Feel..62

Chapter 8: Adding Rhythmic Material to Your Lines..64

Foreword

I first met Danny in his hometown of Rochester and we discussed getting together the following month at my home to talk bass. The low down is that Danny Ziemann is an extremely talented bassist full of creativity, enthusiasm and the utmost respect for the tradition. I am excited that he has taken the time to organize his thoughts on bass line construction for all of us bassists who are full of questions.

The Low Down ends up being much more than a guide to creating jazz bass lines. Danny breaks down the essential elements that make for a great bass player. With extreme clarity *The Low Down* articulates a progressive approach to bass line construction. By emphasizing the need to always go back to the records, Danny has struck the balance between musical thought and feeling, and by doing so has made an extremely valuable contribution to bass instruction.

-Larry Grenadier

Preface

In striving to refine my musicianship, I've always found that I improve most by constantly going back to address the basics. In my teaching, the question students ask most is: "How can I construct my own jazz bass lines?" Teaching bass line construction for many years has caused me to reflect on the essential beginnings of this skill. In all of my teaching experience, the word *how* becomes the driving force of my teaching philosophy: How does this idea work? How do I figure out the right combination of notes? *How* forces you to ask the right questions and seek out answers. Giving you the tools to make your own educated decisions creates a more personalized path to success.

This book represents my approach to constructing bass lines built on the principle of asking *how* an idea fundamentally works and what factors influence it. The formulas and methods will still work on bass guitar, but the Low Down is focused on upright bass for sound, layout, etc. I don't necessarily tell you what to do, rather I ask "*How* can you think about these ideas and apply them to your own playing?" Approaching each factor with this level of attention and detail will help you discover what sounds good to your ear. In my serious pursuit of being an educator, I aim to provide you with comprehensive ways to examine the same details and components that I found relevant for me. Ask the right questions to answer what works for you, your hands, your ears, and your creative vision. This book follows my favored sequence of learning (fundamental sound and layout before line construction) and will continually reinforce concepts mentioned throughout. Don't get too fancy, take your time, and remember that learning the skill of bass line construction is a lifelong pursuit.

There is an accompanying recording available for listening online. Examples with a recording will be marked with a headphone icon. The recordings are not meant to serve as a play-along—read while listening to the recordings to help give further context to each example.

I intend to follow this book with a second volume on bass soloing, bebop line construction, and more layout information. For now, enjoy *The Low Down!*

Chapter 1
The Warm-Up

Having a well constructed and consistent warm up routine is crucial for a number of reasons. It allows you to address physical and philosophical components of upright bass playing. It eases you into playing a physically demanding instrument without developing physical pains (and also keeps you proactive in case they do start). It allows you to foster a healthy and attentive mindset. It can help you to identify if there's something wrong with your instrument (buzzes, open seams, etc). Lastly, a warm-up addresses two of the more personalized pieces to jazz bass playing: your time and your tone.

Addressing time in your warm-up

Bassists (but really every musician) should be generating musical pulse (time + groove) whenever they're playing. If you ask ten musicians to discuss the idea of time, you will receive ten vastly different points of view. Philosophies of time in music can be discussed heavily, but for the purposes of this book they will not be. When warming up it's essential to regularly use a metronome! A metronome forces consistency in your routine. Understand that time and groove are two separate ideas functioning together. Groove can be developed by playing along with records, finding rhythm sections that exemplify what feels you like, and playing with like-minded musicians as often as you can. Time is individually easier to address and can be worked on more exclusively with the metronome. The mechanism for producing a sound happens *before* sound is actually articulated and projected from your instrument. Keeping time is about controlling space and motion in between the beats. Example 1.1 helps clarify the idea of being engaged rhythmically between beats.

Developing your tone

Tone, or sound, is the most distinct identifier of a bassist's playing. The path to developing a personalized sound is lifelong and always being influenced. The importance of sound should be prioritized in any practice or performance situation. There are endless examples bassists on recordings to shape the way you perceive and project your tone. Tone largely informs note choice and line direction (a sustained growl will lead to different note choices than, say, a dry and punchy bounce), and it also heavily impacts the overall shape of the music.

Devote part of your warm-up specifically to the right hand's time and tone production. The left hand makes large contributions to sound as well; the amount of finger pad you use, flat vs curved finger tips, and degree of vibrato will all shape the sustain and color of your note. For the purpose of our warm-up, we will separate the two hands and focus on the unique components of each. This discussion of sound stems from my Three T's philosophy of playing bass: **Time, Tone, and Tunes**. Taste is the honorary fourth T. Having these elements under control ensures more opportunities to play with others.

Before warming up, let's consider three factors in our right hand:

1) Which fingers are you using? Only your pointer finger? Mostly middle finger? Alternating? Third finger too?

The classic way of walking is primarily pointer (index) finger. For two-finger soloing and walking, Christian McBride and John Clayton are examples of bassists who exemplify this technique. From what I've seen, Larry Grenadier uses a good deal of middle finger in his picking, Peter Washington stacks two fingers, and players like Eddie Gomez and Niels-Henning Orsted Pedersen employ three-finger pizzicato.

2) Where do you place your plucking finger? Right at the end of the fingerboard? A little above? Below?

The lower your contact point, the more "thump" you'll produce in your sound, with a higher point of contact giving more "snap" in the articulation. The same articulation isn't appropriate for everything; ballad articulation is different than an up-tempo walking line, which is why experimenting is so important. Having a bag of different articulations and knowing the best context to use them allows you to shape the music most effectively.

3) How much finger are you using? Just the tip of your finger? The whole side?

Once again, the amount of finger you use (paired with its contact point) alters the midrange (body) of your tone, sustain, and the front of your articulation.

Engaging the Right Arm

In addition to the articulating finger, the right arm plays a key role in the production of tone. While the index or middle fingers articulate the note to add a percussive "thump," pulling the string with the right arm engages larger muscle groups to help draw an even bigger sound out of the instrument (similar to the full-arm motion of dragging your arm through a pool of water). Engaging your arm provides two advantages: it draws a larger and fuller sound out of the instrument, and reduces strain on your hands. Your arm length and body size will determine a comfortable amount of movement and how hard to pull the string. I conceptualize the articulating finger as "hook" and use my arm to pull rather than my finger. Your finger should travel along the natural curvature of the fingerboard when articulating and pull right through the string. There should be a roughly 90-120 degree angle made from your wrist to elbow and elbow to shoulder when articulating. Keeping a straight wrist reduces hand injury. Depending on what sound you're going for, more or less arm may be appropriate.

Ultimately, there is no one correct tone: Experiment with these variables in the following exercises to help find what works best for you. All of these factors will noticeably affect your sound. Practice Example 1.1 to address your sound in conjunction with your time:

Example 1.1

1) Set the metronome to 80 bpm, with each pulse indicating a quarter note
2) Play measure #1. After articulating the string, let the note sustain even after moving to the next string. Play for 1 minute.
- Advance to #2
- Advance to #3
- Advance to #4
- Advance to #5

Start this exercise at a *mp-mf* dynamic. Focus on controlling the tonal factors described earlier, particularly the amount of finger used and the contact point on the string. Subtlety and nuance in tone are lost at loud dynamics, and you'll have to first learn to control the clarity of your tone at a soft dynamic before having loud control. The softer you play, the quicker you'll have to pull the string to make it speak. Articulation is the same sensation as snapping your fingers—move too slow and you won't produce any sound. If you can learn to focus your sound at a reasonable dynamic, it will translate better across the spectrum of volume. And, while bassists these days have the luxuries of amps, microphones, and pickups, practice without the amp so you can develop your sound on your own. To quote Ray Brown: "Play the amp, don't let the amp play you!"

Establishing this as a daily routine is meditative—the consistency allows you to focus on important musical elements and establish a positive mood for your session. Since we stand or sit behind our instrument and can't hear accurately how it projects, face your bass in the corner of a room while practicing for immediate feedback of how your instrument sounds.

Increasing hand coordination through your warm-up

The next warm-up technique is a hybrid of two different technical exercises. Example 1.3 uses the chromatic scale (Example 1.2) to focus on articulation and coordination between the left and right hands. The chromatic scale is a versatile tool that can facilitate a lot of practice ideas.

Example 1.2

Learn this as high as you comfortably can. It's a great way to map out upper notes in thumb position. I aim for "G" at the end of the fingerboard before I run out of room on my bass. You can also start this scale on the D, A, and E strings.

Example 1.3

1) Set the metronome to 60 bpm, with each pulse indicating a quarter note.
2) Play the scale in quarter notes, ascending and descending (do not repeat top note).
3) Keep the same tempo, repeating the scale but in eighth notes (variation 1).
   • The eighth notes are **straight**, not swung.
   • Continue examples 2, 3, 4, and 5 without stopping in between.
4) When you've completed all the examples, add ten clicks to the metronome (70bpm) and repeat steps two and three.
5) Continue to increase the bpm until you've reached your limit. From there, increase in 1-3 bpm increments daily.

The metronome only articulates half notes, making it your responsibility to subdivide and make the divisions feel comfortable. The reason to continue without stopping between new subdivisions is to make you instantly feel the new beat. When rhythmic groupings #4 and #5 become too fast, focus on 1-3. This is a systematic way to improve hand coordination, increase your speed, and learn what picking combinations are comfortable for your hands. Practice with one and two fingers. This exercise becomes particularly useful when you start walking up-tempos. For similar exercises in dexterity, play from *Hanon The Virtuoso Pianist*.

Points to consider in practice and playing with others

- On the upright bass, intonation is crucial—you must practice with the bow. Pizzicato has no real center of pitch. Practicing scales, études, and melodies slowly with the bow is the only way to develop a strong sense of pitch and an accurate understanding of the fingerboard. A good bass line with great note choices but bad intonation is a *bad bass line*. Tone and intonation are synonymous—your tone suffers the more out of tune you are. As the bassist, you are the foundation and cannot compromise pitch! This is not much of an issue on electric bass because of the frets.

- The exercises for increasing facility are to develop your chops and strength, but know that having incredible picking accuracy is not a requirement to play the bass. You don't need to play 16th notes at 250bpm to be a successful bassist. There is a growing trend of increased speed and facility but in fact, most of the loved and respected bassists didn't play as fast or note-heavy as today. Taste transcends mindless technique, always. Technique serves to deliver musical ideas, always.

- Don't get caught up in the idea that "high action=big sound." Strings that are too high can choke the sound of the instrument and speed the development of hand pains. Gut strings are normally higher than steel strings because they have a lower tension. Learn to produce your natural sound with a moderate setup, and then make adjustments after developing strength and a clearer concept of tone. Tone is conceived and produced first in the ears.

- In creating your own warm-up, always try to address some form of these elements:
    - Tone (touch, nuance, articulation, intonation)
    - Time
    - Bow

Chapter 2
Developing a Layout of Your Instrument

The exercises in this chapter serve to help you develop a clear layout of the fingerboard. As a bassist, you should in no way be held back by a lack of familiarity with your instrument. No parts of the fingerboard should be off limits, and at no point should you ever be playing and think, "Gee, I don't know what note this is!" Nothing is worse than playing and being totally lost on your instrument. If you're serious about the music, don't let yourself settle for that.

A fundamental understanding of these exercises is key to preventing those nightmare scenarios from ever happening. These exercises will help you fill in the fingerboard through scale and chordal exercises, use open strings to create more (or less) shifting opportunities, and create clear and consistent paths through chord changes. Diligently practice these chord shapes with varying fingerings and reinforce them through all the keys. This is no easy feat, but it won't take long before clear paths and a general layout start to form on the fingerboard.

The point of these exercises is not to develop soloistic chops (although they will develop subsequently), rather the overall goal is to give yourself the means to make the most informed note choices. Technical proficiency ultimately equals having more options available on the instrument. Avoiding certain areas of your instrument would be like a pianist avoiding entire areas of the keyboard. Achieving success in understanding your instrument means providing the most supportive note choice. Technique should only be addressed as a means of furthering your musicianship. Really, the whole point is this: great facility means better support and informed note choices.

Mapping out diatonic 7ths

These exercises explore possibilities within the major and minor scales. Every note of the major scale implies a 7th chord of some type:

Example 2.1

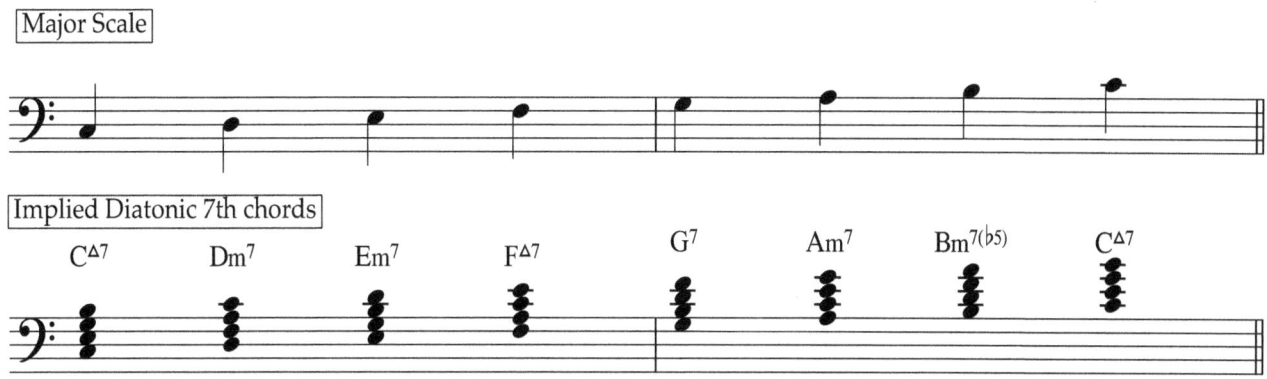

These chords can be arpeggiated to create a more complete layout of the fingerboard. There are at least three different ways of fingering these sounds: Explore them and see what is most comfortable for your hand shape.

Example 2.2

To highlight different points of chordal connectivity, play the arpeggios these eight ways:

Example 2.3

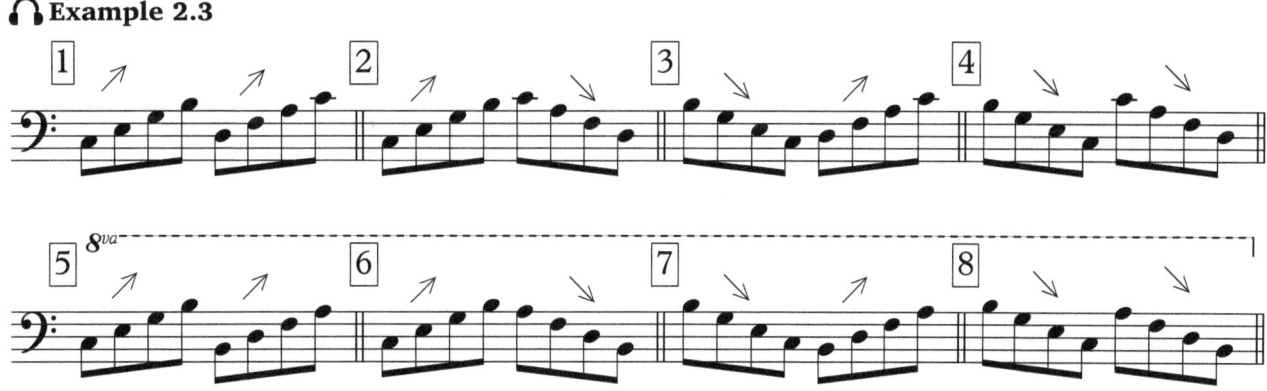

Set the metronome to 60bpm, with one pulse indicating a quarter note. Arpeggiate the diatonic chords, starting with pattern 1 in Example 2.3. When you reach the top of the first octave, descend continuing the same pattern. When comfortable, repeat with variations 2-4. Continue with 5-8, but notice that they start in thumb position. Not all keys will begin in thumb position. If you're not comfortable playing in thumb position, play the highest arpeggio you can for that particular key and then descend from there.

15

Next, try different interval combinations. The first example follows the interval pattern of **1-7-3-5**. The second is a bit more complicated: **1-7-3-5**, **5-3-7-1**. You can apply these patterns to all of the arpeggios. Be as creative as possible.

Example 2.4

Most importantly, these chordal exercises should be practiced in all 12 keys. Pick a key each week, starting with C, and travel around the circle of fourths. The rationale is this: because so many keys share common chords (C Major and F Major both contain A Minor chords for example), by the time you've finished all twelve keys you've reinforced many of the same sounds all over the instrument in different contexts. Some keys may be more difficult than others due to a lack of open strings—learn to feel the shapes of the chords.

The same treatment of chords can be applied to minor keys, using Melodic Minor as our parent scale:

Example 2.5

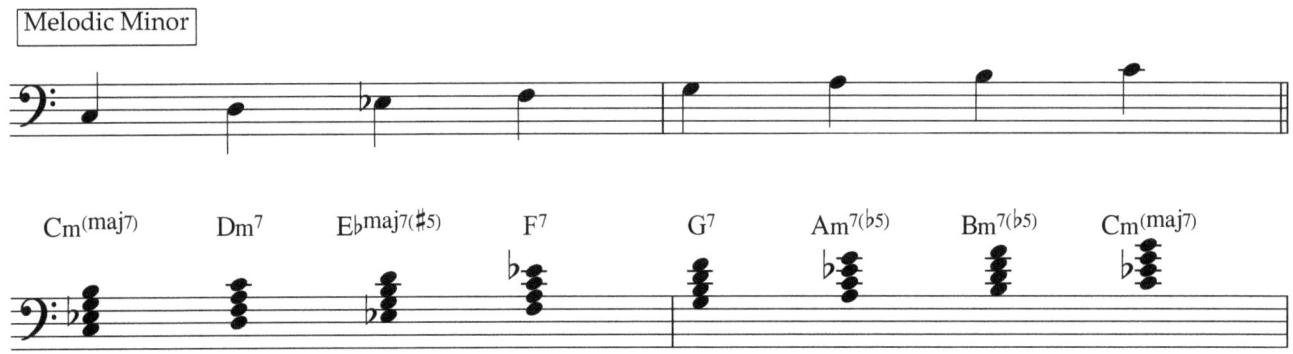

Minor arpeggios can be extracted in the same way as major, and should be practiced the same 8 ways after demonstrating command of the major key. The differences between Melodic Minor and Major are very small, so look for the little detail changes.

Example 2.6

Here's one more exercise to help fill out the minor sounds. Practice in the same eight ways you would the other exercises. Because diminished chords are symmetrical, there are only so many keys and variations before you're reinforcing the same sounds.

Example 2.7

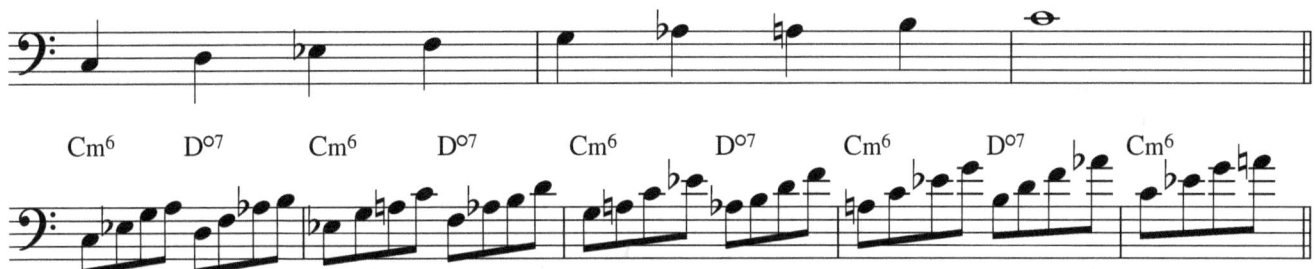

Establishing a plan for practice

As the bass is tuned in fourths, I prefer taking my practice through the circle of fourths. I'm a fan of the "key-a-week" method. Applying this method to the exercises above will make for a systematic routine with tangible learning goals. A good routine might contain the following:

    5-10 minutes of open strings/sound warm-up
    20-30 minutes of Diatonic 7th chords

Begin with Example 2.2 in C Major. Once you're comfortable, play it in the Parallel Minor key. There are many shared chords, so transitioning between tonalities won't be as difficult as learning a new key entirely. As you become more comfortable with major/minor, try Example 2.7. This should be a bit easier as diminished sounds lay nicely on the bass. Don't worry about speed; a slow but consistent tempo is better than a fast and jagged execution.

If you can't accomplish this all in one week, don't worry—a key every two or three weeks might be a more feasible goal. The more keys you have under your fingers, the easier the exercises become—you'll begin to notice a lot of similarities in shapes and patterns. Practice the Major, Melodic Minor, and Diminished patterns all in the same key before moving forward. You can also gradually increase metronome speed as you become more familiar with the patterns.

Building triads vertically

Traveling vertically and playing positionally on the fingerboard is to your absolute advantage. Guitarists exploit this and have triads built right into the open tuning of their guitar—DGB (inverted G Major triad). They can bar their finger to easily grab numbers of triads. We can take the idea of vertical triadic shapes and find ways to use them on our own instrument: **triad pairs** over dominant sounds, ii-V-I's, etc. For example, here's a GMaj7#11 sound using G&A triads:

Example 2.8

Play through as many inversions ascending and descending as you can. The goal is to try and use the A, D, and G strings exclusively. This increases speed and limits the amount of shifting. It also creates block shapes to fill in the fingerboard similarly to the diatonic patterns. Stacking patterns makes articulation easier on the right hand, shown in Example 2.9:

🎧 **Example 2.9**

Just as with the Diatonic 7th chords, create your own interval patterns to practice. You do not have to start on the same chord tone in each triad you can break them up however you'd like.

You can use triadic shapes to help you navigate through ii-V-I's. Example 2.10 is based on measures 3-5 of "I Remember You":

Example 2.10

This can help you sequence through cycling and patterned chord changes ("Have You Met Miss Jones," etc). The advantage is minimal shifting while making a very clear harmonic statement.

Using open strings

Open strings are the secret to navigating the instrument freely—this applies to walking and especially solo lines. They allow us to continue line shape without having to shift endlessly and break an alternating 1-2 fingering in the right hand. If you don't play bass guitar, I highly recommend borrowing (or buying) one and practicing these patterns on there as well. This helps to strengthen the visual layout.

First, pick a scale/mode (C Lydian Dominant, for example):

Example 2.11

Establish block position (no shifting, just play across the neck) on the E string, 2nd finger on C, and attempt to use every open string without shifting. When you play an open string, let it ring even after you continue to play the next note. You may need to shift for the last note of the scale.

🎧 **Example 2.12**

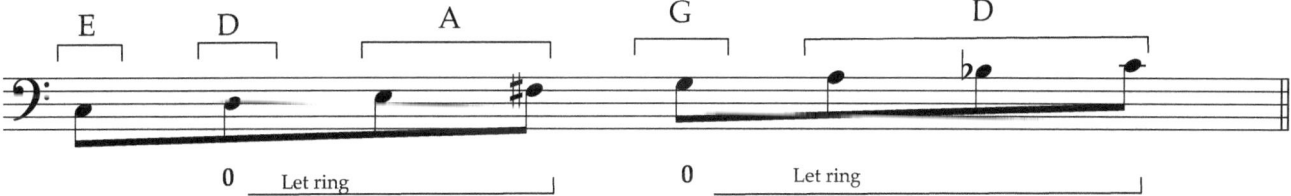

Exercise 2.12 addresses two important ideas: it reinforces strong left hand shape (through tunneling) and breaks down the notion of "higher placed finger equals higher pitch." By letting the higher positioned string ring while continuing the scale on a lower string, you're forced to shift in a way that seems counter-intuitive. Many soloists exploit open strings to continue their idea and line direction. The same can be true for bass lines. Learning to play these sounds vertically will help facilitate easier navigation through the instrument. This exercise will work on any scale that can use an open string.

Discovering scale paths

Bassists often rely on playing their scales in half position or first position and then shifting up the G string to continue additional octaves. While this may be most appropriate if you're playing repertoire with the bow and need tonal clarity, it's not very practical for us. There are generally three directions to conceptualize scale shapes on the bass:

1) Linear   2) Vertical   3) Combination of both (hybrid)

This first scale climbs all the way up the E string:

Example 2.13

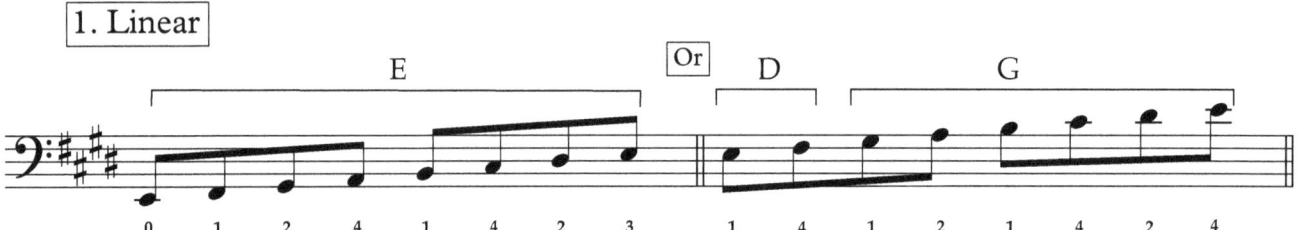

The second scale makes use of the A string as a pivot to finish traveling in a mostly vertical (block) direction:

Example 2.14

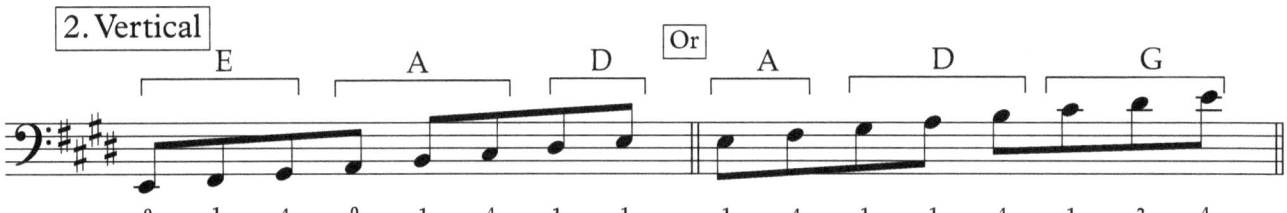

The last scale is a hybrid of both approaches, making more of a "zig-zag" shape through the instrument:

Example 2.15

When practicing scale paths...
- There is no scale fingering that is more "right" than another. These are also not the only three ways you can play scales. Including traveling up and down just one string, you should be able to find about 5-6 independent scale paths.
- Use open strings as much as you can to create new options.
- Practice these SLOWLY and with the bow, not just pizzed. Focus on your sound and intonation.
- Practice all of your scales this way—major, minor, modes, etc.

Points to consider in practice and playing with others

- If you play with poor intonation, your visual layout of the instrument won't be clear. Hearing a line and being able to play it accurately can only happen if you practice in a way that reinforces strong pitch. If you can't hear an idea because of poor intonation, the best you'll be able to do is approximate shapes that you're seeing, not lines you're actually hearing.

- Practice these exercises with the bow. Quiet, slow practice with the bow is the most accurate way to develop your sense of intonation. The center of pitch in a pizzed note is not as stable as a bowed note.

- The point of technical proficiency is to help you make the most musically informed note choices at all times.

- The ability to solo well comes secondarily to having a solid understanding of note paths and walking line construction. While these exercises do help develop your soloing chops, approach it for now as a way to help your walking abilities.

- These exercises are here to help you think about developing your own personalized layout. Everyone's hand shape is different, with some ideas working easier than others. There is no one way to view the instrument, so take the time to develop your own vision.

Chapter 3
Fundamental Bass Line Construction

This chapter presents you with the most basic ways to conceive walking bass lines and can guide you successfully through most tunes you'll encounter. Before we dive into the nitty-gritty of constructing a bass line it's important to talk about what a good bass line actually does. What's the purpose of a bass line? In its most fundamental role, the bass is an instrument of function—the bassist, through careful note and rhythmic choices, outlines harmony, directs/marks form, and generates rhythmic groove & pulse. A bassist has the ability to elevate the entire level of the band through careful listening and attentive note choice. Every musician has their own way in which they address these tasks and takes care of business. In every great bassist's playing, elements of strong **time** and **tone** are attended to with the same attention to detail. It should be clear by now that creating a feeling of comfortable time and developing a well-developed tonal palette are fundamental to your role. Though every bassist phrases their rhythm differently, harmonic note choice is what gives a bassist the most amount of "say" in a musical situation.

My approach works by providing five specific and sequential formulas that layer your understanding of how a line is created. The only prior information needed is knowledge of triads and sevenths (one reason for the exercises in previous chapters). I've included a guide that explains chord formulas on the next page.

For now, write lines using only quarter notes with no additional rhythmic activity. Adding rhythmic variations in bass lines first requires careful note choice and a firm understanding of harmonic line construction. Adding rhythmic activity will be discussed later in Chapter 7. This chapter includes many examples of bass lines to demonstrate and reinforce understanding. The examples are based on Blues chord changes and the chord changes from "Autumn Leaves"—pedagogically speaking, they are the most straightforward changes to begin writing bass lines with. "Autumn Leaves" has two keys, in this case Bb Major and G Minor; both are relative as they share the same key signature and will use all of the chord types discussed in this book. In hopes of reinforcing vertical and linear harmony, these construction formulas provide a nice balance of lines based on arrival points and lines that are more intervallic. **Vertical harmony** addresses the chords in a more arpeggiated way, aiming to articulate all the important chord tones in each measure. **Linear Harmony** might ignore particular chord tones while aiming for a greater target point. A combination of both truly results in the most melodic lines. A more thorough explanation of arrival points and advanced line construction will be addressed later in this book.

While the formula remains the same, some chords can be notated in different ways.

Formulas	Examples
Major7, Maj7, M7, $\triangle$7: 1-3-5-7	CMajor7, CMaj7, CM7, C$^{\triangle 7}$
minor7, min7, m7, -7: 1-b3-5-b7	Cminor7, Cmin7, Cm7, C-7
(*Dominant 7*) **7**: 1-3-5-b7	C7
min7(b5), m7(b5), ø7: 1-b3-b5-b7	Cmin7(b5), Cm7(b5), C^{ø7}

These formulas are based on the major scale that corresponds to the root of the chord, and a flat symbol indicates that a pitch should be lowered by a half step. Sometimes, lowering a pitch by a half step will mean going from a natural to a flat, and other times it may mean going from sharp to a natural or even a flat to a double flat. For example, with a root of D, a major 7 chord would be spelled D, F sharp, A, C sharp, matching the key signature of two sharps in the D major scale. A Dmin7b5 chord would be spelled D, F natural, A flat, C natural, with scale degrees 3, 5, and 7 all a half step lower than the pitches of the D major scale. With a root of D flat, a major 7 chord would be spelled D flat, F, A flat, C, matching the key signature of five flats in the D flat major scale. A Dbmin7b5 chord would be spelled D flat, F flat (enharmonic equivalent of E natural), A double flat (enharmonic equivalent of G natural), C flat (enharmonic equivalent of B natural). The example below spells these chords out.

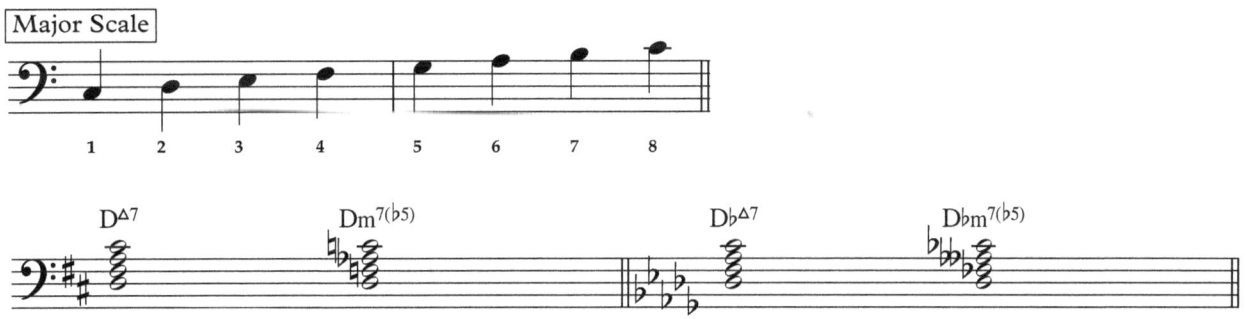

Familiarize yourself with the following terms:

R = Root
CT = Chord Tone
PT = Passing Tone (or non-harmonic tone)
HS = Half Step
WS = Whole Step

The **root** is the foundational note of the chord (the "1") in which other harmonic information is based from. A **chord tone** is any note that is a part of the basic chord formula (with alterations to fit the quality). A **passing tone**, or, **non-harmonic tone** (both can generally be interchanged) is a note that does not relate to the chord—it is usually a chromatic note used to connect chord tones or to the root of the next chord. A **half step** is a stepwise chromatic interval, and a **whole step** is the distance of two half steps.

Method 1: Chord tones

R CT CT CT

Method 1 is the most elementary way to create a bass line. Each measure begins with the root and contains only notes available from that chord. If there are two chords per measure, follow the root with a chord tone to the next root. This is the method I learned first, and I still use it in my playing daily. Constructing a bass line using only chord tones ensures that you have total control of the harmony and should be the starting point for any line you create. What you may lose in variety you'll gain in melodic clarity and ease of movement around the bass. Any great bassist will be able to play a line using nothing but chord tones and still keep it interesting. This will work on all standards you encounter, and in fact may even work best on more difficult tunes with a lot of changes (or ones that move quickly), including "Fee Fi Fo Fum," "Giant Steps," "Stablemates," etc.

Here's a bass line using the all-chord-tone approach with the chosen chord tones labeled:

Example 3.1

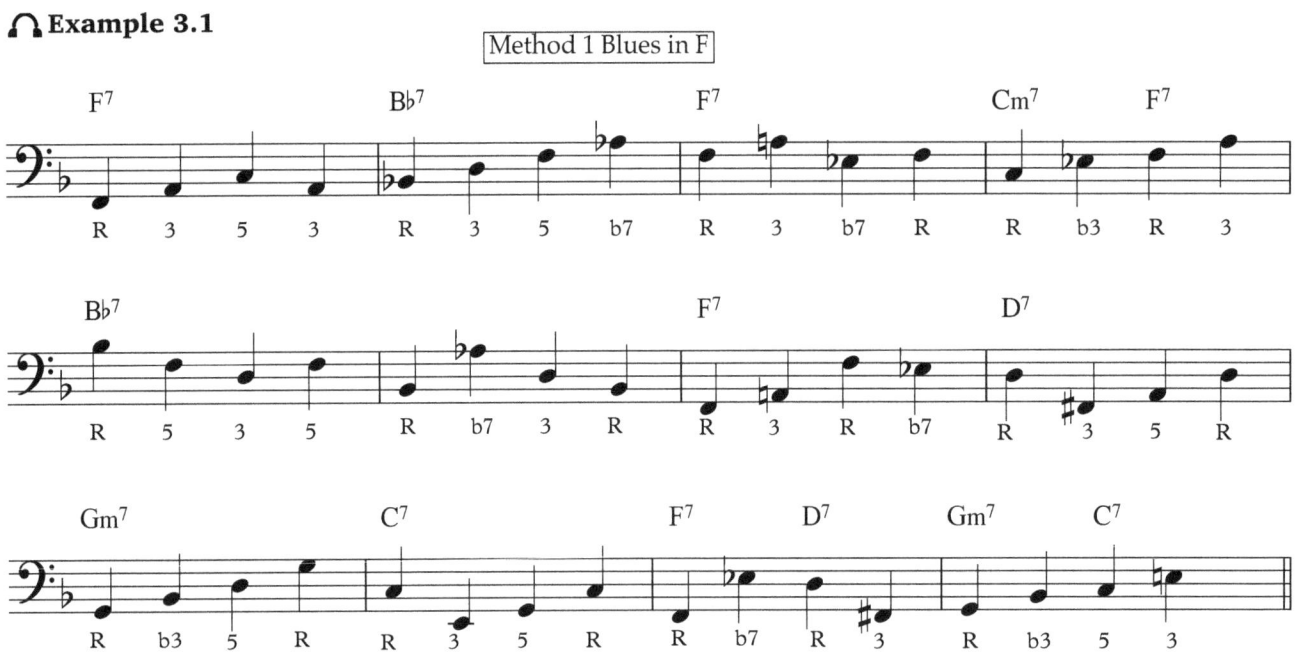

As you can see, each chord is outlined and the harmony is articulated clearly.

Here's an example based on the first eight bars from "Autumn Leaves":

🎧 **Example 3.2**

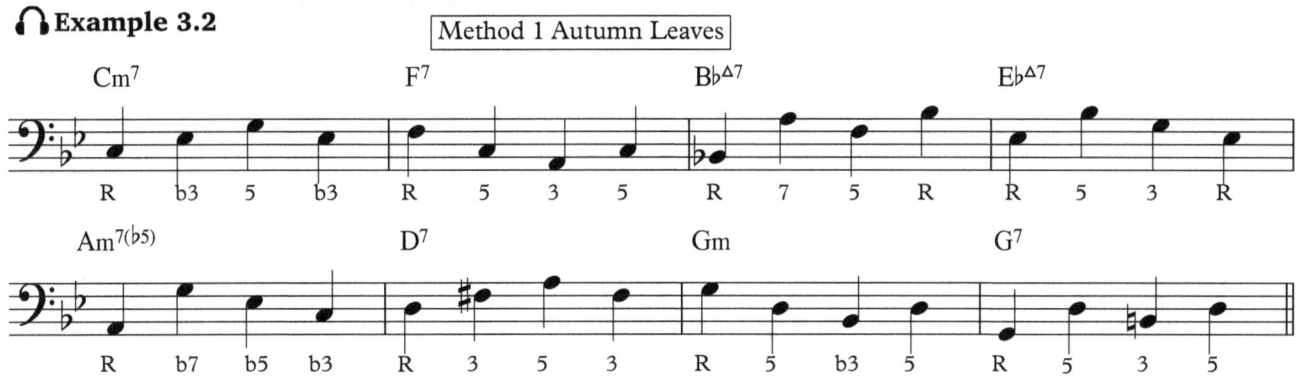

Conveniently, the voice leading (the melodic transition from one chord to the next, which is smoothest when using half steps or whole steps instead of wide leaps) will often occur naturally with chord tones. ii-V-I is the most common progression in jazz music—familiarize yourself with these progressions and how they function. Arpeggiate them in your practice. In ii-V-I progressions (Cm7-F7-BbMaj7 for example) the 7th of the ii chord moves to the 3rd of the V chord, with the 3rd of the ii chord naturally becoming the 7th of the V chord:

Example 3.3

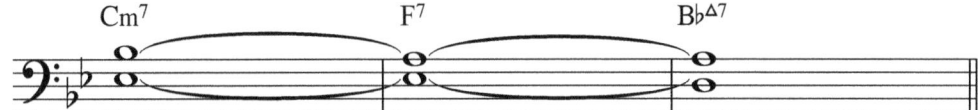

When coming across a ii-V-I in major or minor, you can play the chordal 7th (of the ii chord) on beat 4, followed by the 3rd (of the V chord) on the downbeat. Make sure to follow the non-root downbeat with a root and chord tones to continue the rest of the formula. We call this a **delayed root resolution** (which will be talked about a bit later). Example 3.4 demonstrates how to delay the root and naturally arpeggiate ii-V-I's over Autumn Leaves.

🎧 **Example 3.4**

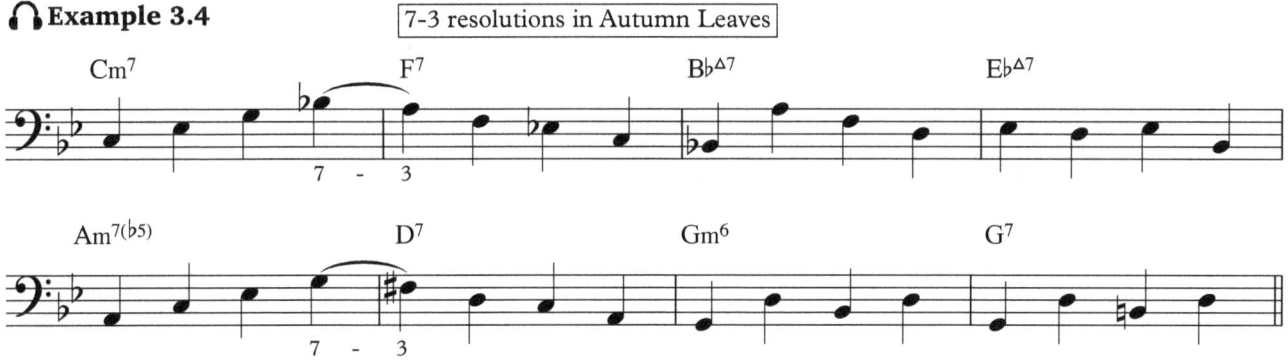

Pick a few standards and write as many bass lines as you can. Some accessible first tunes include: "Just Friends," "All the Things You Are," "Autumn Leaves," "On the Sunny Side of the Street," "All of Me," "Take the A Train." I'm not the biggest advocate of the Real Book as I believe tunes are best learned by ear, but when you're starting to write bass lines it can be a comprehensive source to find tunes for practicing. The best way to learn tunes, however, is by going straight to the source and listen to recordings! Ear training should always be at the forefront of one's musical studies, and learning tunes/transcribing from records is a great way to engage the aural side of learning. Once you've familiarized yourself with Method 1, read about Method 2 to see how one slight variation can change your line direction.

Method 2: Chord tones with a passing tone

This method uses chord tones on beats **1, 2, and 3** but replaces beat 4 with a **passing tone** either a half step above or below the root of the following chord. This method follows Method 1 of constructing bass lines as it only alters one note. The advantage of bass lines that follow this method is continued clarity of harmony with added variation in line direction. Your bass lines will become vertical and linear in nature.

Example 3.5 uses Blues in F with the chosen chord tones and passing tones labeled underneath. Sometimes, the passing tone and the chord tone are the same—I've highlighted in parentheses when this happens. These instances are more likely to occur when there is a quick ii-V-I of two beats per chord.

🎧 **Example 3.5**

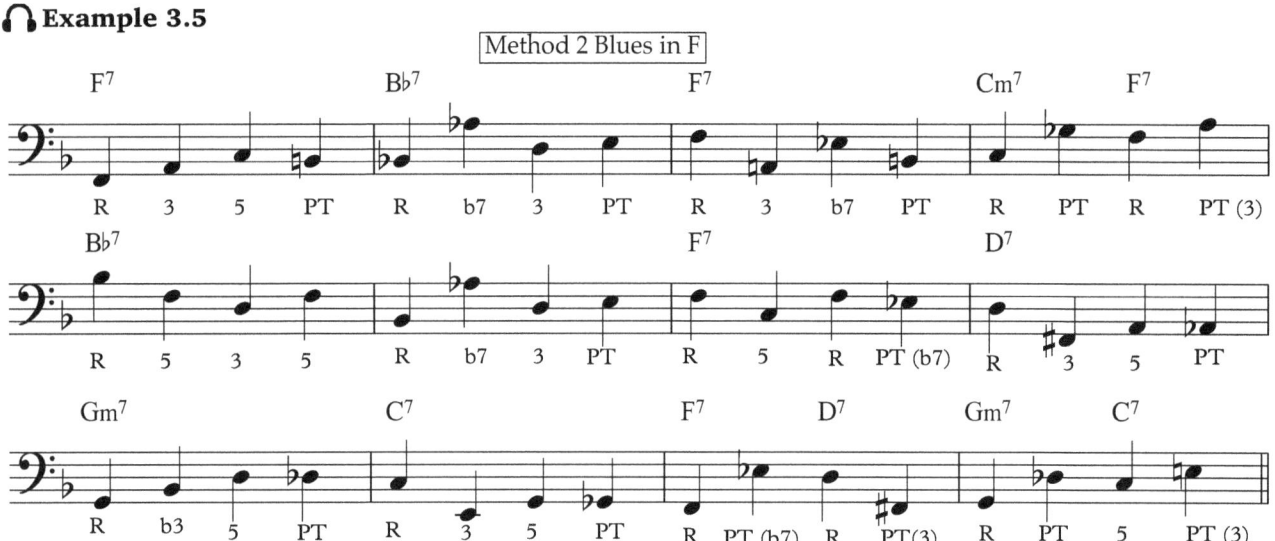

Example 3.6 demonstrates a bass line using Method 2, based off of the changes from "Autumn Leaves." Again, I've highlighted when the passing tone and chord tone are the same.

🎧 **Example 3.6**

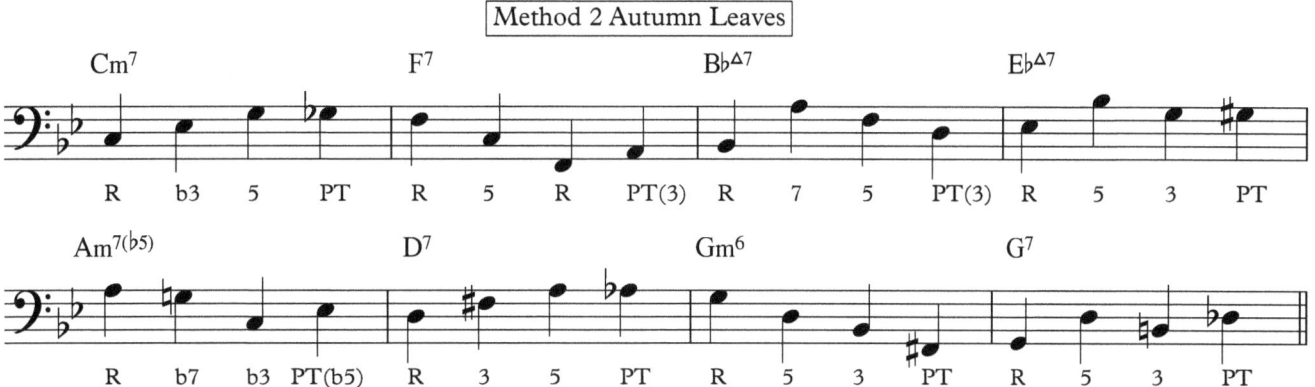

Write bass lines with the same diligence as you did using Method 1. You may end up using a lot of the same material; that's OK. When looking for differences, take notice of how the overall shape in the line changes as beat four is altered. This is one of the most common ways of creating bass lines that you'll learn—listen to recordings and you'll hear an abundance of these types of lines. Using Method 2 in conjunction with other methods creates the best variety in your lines. When comfortable with Method 2, explore Method 3.

Method 3: Adding more passing tones

$$R \quad HS \rightarrow HS \rightarrow HS \rightarrow | \quad R$$

This method adds more passing tones by approaching each root from three half-steps above (or below) the subsequent root. You can navigate to or from any chord using this method. Note: **This is not the best way to outline harmony as it exclusively emphasizes the arrival on beat one.** It is a simple way to change direction and overall line shape when used in conjunction with Methods 1 and 2.

Here's a Blues in F that demonstrates Method 3:

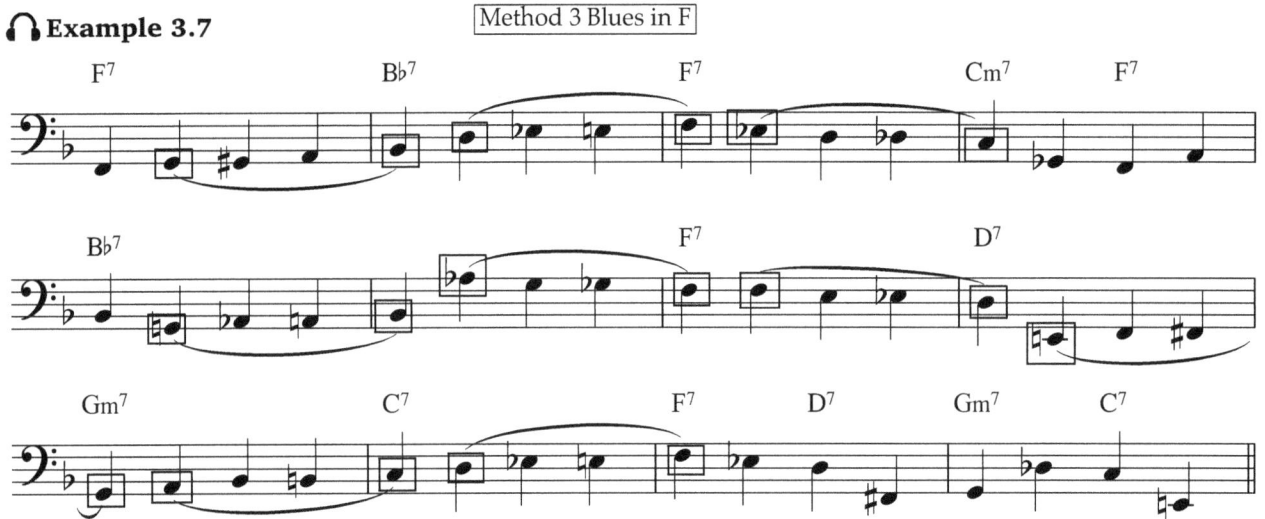

Except for measure four with the quick ii-V progression, every measure contains this passing tone formula. Example 3.8 demonstrates arrivals using the first 8 measure from "Autumn Leaves":

Use Method 3 sparingly—chromatic arrivals are like a spice and should not be your predominant means of articulating harmony. The use of Method 3 should be in conjunction with the more tonally stable methods, and it is most effective when approaching an important harmonic arrival in the form. Write a few bass lines using nothing but this method and you'll see how little harmonic support is actually being provided. Method 3 merely provides more emphasis to your pillar arrival points and changes your line's direction. To further expand upon targeting arrival points, move on to Method 4.

Method 4: Descending scale arrival (in Major and Minor keys)

| R | CT | WS → WS → | R |

| R | CT | HS → WS → | R |
(Minor Keys)

Method 4 works by outlining scale degrees 3-2-1 of the following chord. This adds emphasis to the root of the chord without introducing outside chromaticism. If you are approaching a Major or Dominant sound, you would choose the first formula. If you are approaching a Minor sound, you would choose the second formula.

In a Major ii-V7-I progression, Cm7-F7-BbMaj7 for example, you can approach all three chords with the relevant formulas from Method 4: BbMaj7 and F7 (I and V) would both be approached by the first formula, and Cm7 (ii) would be approached the second formula.

In a minor ii°-V-i progression, *you should approach only the i chord and use the second formula*—if you approach any other chords in the progression, you'll be adding notes outside the chord/key and harmonically they won't sound right (unless your chord player voices them with specific extensions). You can still use Method 3 to approach these chords.

🎧 **Example 3.9**

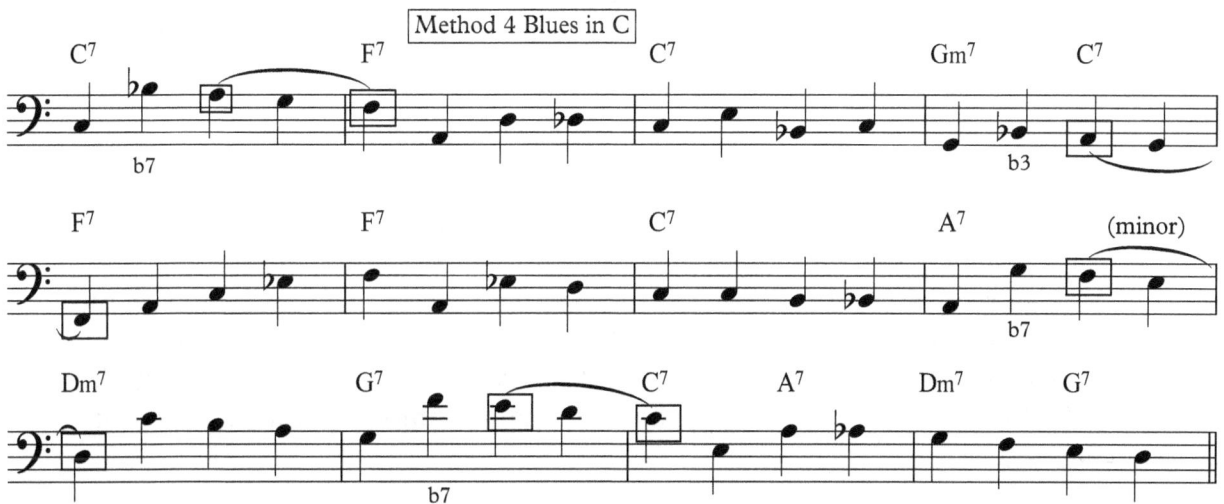

Here's an example using the chord changes "Autumn Leaves." Look for the 3-2-1 approach in major and minor.

🎧 Example 3.10

Note that in both examples, the chord tone that precedes the WS movement is commonly the 7th.

Additional mini-methods

I label these next few points "mini-methods." They are enough material to create a walking line, but are extremely effective devices commonly used by bassists.

Mini Method 1

The first mini-method (labeled as 5a) is the use of **doubled notes**. It's just what the name implies—two of the same consecutive note. Usually the doubled note starts on the root or 5th and can continue as long as you'd like. They're most effective when following a guide tone line. Many bass line transcription you come across will have examples of this. Example 3.11 highlights doubled notes in the first four measures of a blues:

Example 3.11

Mini Method 2

The second mini-method was briefly mentioned in Method 1: **delayed root resolution.** When properly resolving the naturally occurring 7ths to 3rds in your walking line, you've created a delayed root resolution as you're replacing the root on the downbeat with the chordal 3rd. This idea isn't exclusive to just ii-V-I resolutions—you can use a delayed resolution anywhere with good taste, of course. It's most effective when you can use it in the middle of a line and not when arriving at a landmark harmonic point (like measure 7 of "Autumn Leaves").

When delaying the arrival of a root it should still be addressed somewhere in the measure to give context. Beat 2 works well to release tension quickly, but as long as you address it somewhere it's okay, unless your voice leading has a greater target point. This will be discussed in Chapter 6. The point is, do not get too carried away and lose the function of your role!

Example 3.12

Notice the resolution points are thirds and sevenths. The interval between beats 4 and 1 of the following measure is still a half step, except for BbMaj7 to EbMaj7. In the last measure I resolve the root on beat 3.

Mini Method 3

The third mini-method is making **V-I resolutions** to your I chord in major or minor. Look for any opportunity to make these cadences in your bass lines. This would be characterized as using the 5th of the key you're aiming for on beat 4 before the targeted root. Example 4.13 demonstrates this:

Example 3.13

This also stresses an important concept in bass line understanding: *in a ii-V-I, you're already in the I key from the moment you start the ii chord*. If you treat the last measure as a large V-I cadence, it makes for functionally stronger bass lines. This is another tool at your disposal to enhance the clarity of your note choices.

Mini Method 4

The last mini method is the **Tritone Substitution**, a powerful tool used for creating bass lines. A tritone substitution *only function with Dominant chords*, and you can use it by replacing the root of a dominant chord with a new root a tritone (6 half steps) away. For example, G7 would become Db7. The 3rds and 7ths remain the same even when replacing the root, leaving the functionality of the Dominant chord unaffected— both G7 and Db7 contain the necessary F and B(Cb) for resolving to CMaj7. The advantage of having two options is added harmonic color; some melodies and solos may benefit from this reharmonization choice. Again, this only works with Dominant Chords.

This is an easy way to add variety in the direction of your lines but don't substitute them all the time. Often times if you hear a different sound when playing the Dominant chord, it's a tritone substitution. Example 3.14 demonstrates the Tritone Substitution in mm. 27-28 of Autumn Leaves:

Example 3.14

Finally, reusing material can be seen as taboo, but it shouldn't be. Many bassists, particularly one of my favorites Sam Jones, will often reuse the same patterns in the spots of their bass lines. It's not a crime to reuse material. Really, you should be more concerned with the following: Am I conveying the harmony clearly? How does it feel? Am I playing with a good sound? Am I facilitating the creativity of others? Forcing creativity into a bass line will most likely detract from the functionality of it. Being creative only comes from a solid understanding of what you're trying to enhance in the first place. Always aim for functionality first. Learn the language, and the eventually the freedom to be able to speak within the confines of a tune will come (with diligent practice).

Sample bass lines

Here's three choruses of an F Blues using Methods 1-4 and the additional mini-methods. There will be two versions of the same bass line: one as-is and one marked with annotations/accompanying analysis. Any of the methods used will be noted underneath that particular measure. See what you can find before looking at the analysis and listen along with the recording.

For your reference:

Method 1: R CT CT CT
Method 2: R CT CT PT
Method 3: R CT HS HS
Method 4: R WS WS WS
Mini-Method 1: Doubled Notes (labeled MM1)
Mini-Method 2: Delayed Root Resolution (labeled MM2)
Mini-Method 3: V-I Resolution (labeled MM3)
Mini-Method 4: Tritone Substitution (labeled MM4)

🎧 **Example 3.15**

33

Example 3.16

I tried to use each method equally. Sometimes Method 1 will be the same as Method 2 (measure 7). Take notice of where I only used the V chord instead of the ii chord (in measure 4 of the form and 12 usually). Instances of Method 1 being the same Method 3 (F7-D7-Gm7-C7) can occur too.

Here's a bass line based on the chord changes of "Autumn Leaves" unanalyzed, followed by an analyzed version:

Example 3.17

Autumn Leaves Combined Methods

Example 3.18

Points to consider in practice and playing with others

- After you write a bass line, play it on your instrument. Your lines will always be guided by what's comfortable for your hand. You might try something and discover it doesn't feel comfortable or intuitive. If you find something that does turn out to be comfortable, it might influence your overall conceptual thinking in another direction.

- Practice outlining ii-V-I progressions (connecting 3rds and 7ths) in your lines when playing in a group. It will always sound good and reinforces your understanding of voice leading. Consider making ii-V-I arpeggios a part of your warm-up until you're more comfortable with them.

- Learn to play the melodies of these tunes. You should know what you're supposed to be accompanying. A number of tunes use chord tones exclusively in the melody ("All The Things You Are") and you don't want to double them in your bass line. Your goal is to create a bass-note melody that provides support and added interest to the music.

- One of our roles is to help control **tension and release** in the music through the use of rhythmic devices, harmonic choices, or both. Bach was one of the masters of tension and release in music. When walking bass lines we establish tension, ultimately releasing the tension at a point of harmonic stability. Using a passing tone on beat 4 (or passing tones towards the following root) increases tension, with the release of this tension happening on the following stable chord tone. Many leading tones (degrees 5-1, 7-1, b2-1, etc) that control the release of tension are already naturally occurring chord tones. And often times, by beat 4, I'm no longer concerned about the chord I'm playing—I'm more concerned about where it's headed to and how I can release the tension of the phrase I've created.

- Write out a lot of bass lines. Buy or print blank sheet music and formulate as many as you can with a variety of standards. Bassists will play tens of thousands of notes on every gig, multiple times a week. Much of the walking vocabulary I use now is still rooted in what I learned from the beginning. Good vocabulary will stick with you forever and be YOUR vocabulary.

- Play along with recordings. If you learn a tune, write a bass line out and play along with a recording of someone else doing it. It doesn't matter if there's already a bass player—it'll give you a chance to play with a drummer and contextualize what you've written. You can turn down the bass knob on your stereo if you really are distracted by what's going on.

- Play your written bass lines with a metronome articulating first 1&3 and then 2&4. Walking with beats 1&3 articulated on the metronome helps to anchor your time and hold you responsible for the swing feel. 2&4 helps to accents the swing feel automatically like a hi-hat. Practicing with the metronome both ways will help you be aware of subtleties in how you phrase time and groove.

Chapter 4
Rhythm Changes

Rhythm Changes refer to the progression from George Gershwin's song "I Got Rhythm." These changes are characterized by a I-VI-ii-V motion in the A sections, with cycling Dominant 7th chords starting with III7 for the B section. Two things make this form difficult: both the harmonic rhythm and tempo are brisk. What's challenging is also what makes it fun—rhythm changes present many opportunities to play long, melodic lines and play intervallically in block position. During fast tempos, having the economy to play changes without much left hand effort is imperative to lasting through a whole tune. This discipline is useful for playing other fast-paced tunes including "Cherokee," "The Song Is You," etc. Through this study of rhythm changes, our focus will further expand upon vertical and linear harmony.

The vertical approach

A sections:

In regards to energy exertion, the most economical way to approach rhythm changes is using Methods 1&2: a chord tone approach, or, mostly chord tones with few passing tones. As the harmony remains in the tonic (I) key during A sections (with a momentary shift to IV), smooth voice leading to almost any chord tone with very few passing tones occurs. Delayed root resolutions also work nicely when the harmony is mostly diatonic and static. In these instances you can play the root on beat 2; this facilitates smoother linear voice leading. Example 4.1 demonstrates this delayed root resolution line:

🎧 **Example 4.1**

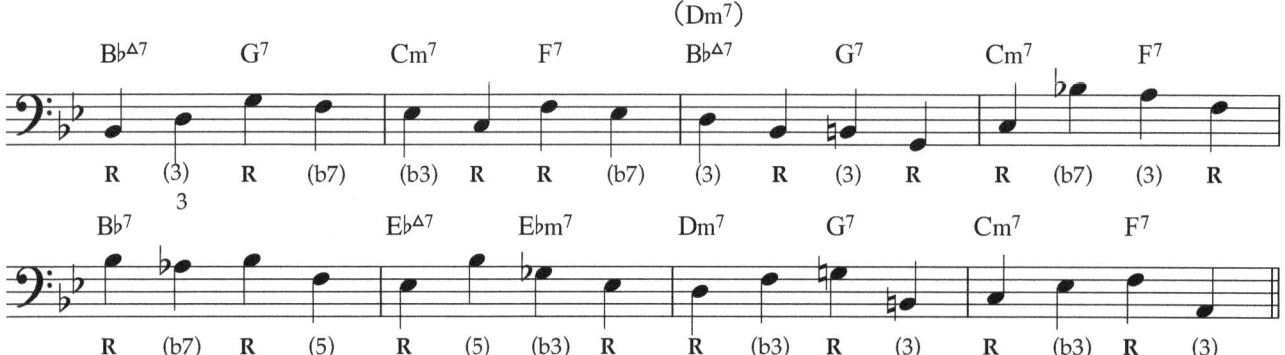

In measure 3 I include the option of using Dmin7. In measure 3 *only,* you can use either BbMaj7 (I) or Dm7 (iii7) for the first chord. Both chords contain similar chord tones and function the same in this instance. This is a simple way to add variety in root movement.

38

Many of the passing tones are chordal 3rds and 7ths. 3rds and 7ths exist in close proximity on the bass, allowing convenient voice leading for the left hand. Every note in this example is a chord tone—you don't need to be fancy to properly convey harmony.

Example 4.2 shows another way to connect these chord changes, this time using passing tones to connect the roots. Notice how sometimes the passing tones will conflict with chord tones (Ab over BbMaj7 in measure three).

🎧 Example 4.2

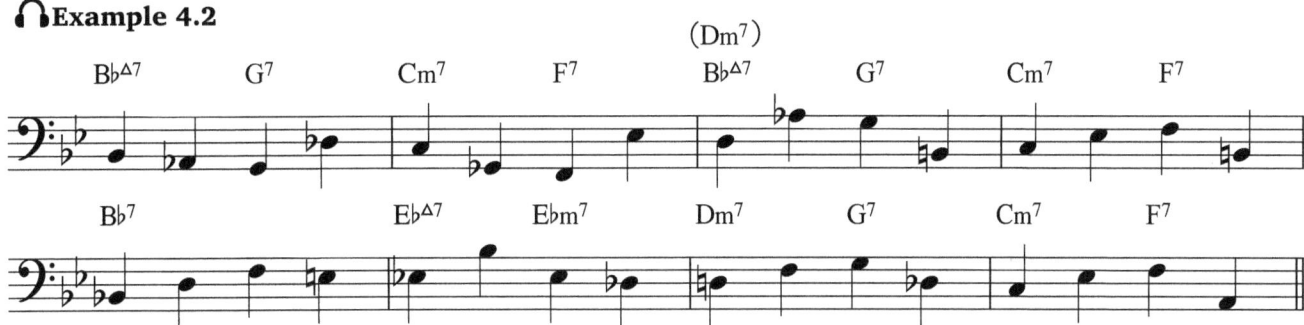

While you are required to shift more in this example, the shifting adds variety without much extra work. There are countless ways to connect these chords together using different passing tones. As previously stated, shape and content is guided to some extent by what's comfortable for your hand size. Find patterns that accommodate your left hand and incorporate them into your playing.

The bridge:

The bridge consists of dominant chords cycling in fourths starting with III7. The harmonic rhythm slows, providing more time to map out the direction of your line. All methods from the previous chapter will be useful in helping choose appropriate notes. Here's an eight bar sample of the bridge—what walking approaches do you see?

🎧 Example 4.3

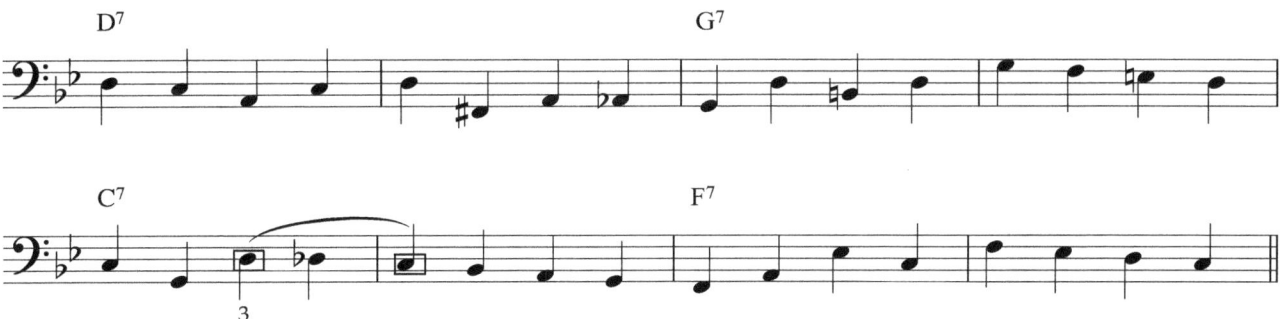

I highlighted one instance of Method 3 to show how it can be used to re-articulate the root of the same chord.

Don't forget about doubled notes either; they work especially well on rhythm changes. As rhythm changes are commonly called at jam sessions, they are often played in different keys and typically go on for a while (to allow everyone a chance to solo)—be prepared to walk. Working out patterns that are comfortable now helps so you're not stuck finding material while playing.

The linear approach

In this section, **Target Notes** and aiming for arrival points from a greater distance away will be explored further. Using **Bebop Scales** can help explore this idea further. Bebop scales work by adding an additional note to a major scale, either between scale degrees 5 and 6 (for Major Bebop), or scale degrees b7-8 (Dominant Bebop). This extra note gives you eight rather than seven pitches, meaning that moving up and down the scale with stepwise motion allows you to continually place chord tones on strong beats, leaving non-chord tones on weak beats. They are an introduction to longer walking phrases, and in this case will work over measures 1-5 and 5-7 of rhythm changes. You can start this scale on degrees 1, 3, or 5 and still voice lead through the I-VI-ii-V progression successfully.

The harmony dictates what scale you would use. Maj7, 6/9, or pentatonic chords are associated with the Major Bebop scale. Dominant chords are associated with the Dominant Bebop scale. Notice what chord tones are emphasized on beats 1 and 3 (strong beats).

Example 4.4

A sections:

Example 4.5 shows how the bebop scale addresses harmony starting on the root, 3rd, and 5th of the scale. In general, I descend the scale more although ascending works well too. You can continue descending into measure three, but in this case, you'll eventually need to move to a higher octave to continue the line direction (unless you are playing this on 5 string electric bass or piano/organ). In variation #2, I changed the quality of G7 to Gm7. Either are acceptable for Rhythm Changes.

Example 4.5

I labeled the examples with a two-tiered system—the top tier labels the chord tones that naturally align vertically with the scale, and the bottom tier represents what scale degrees occur when approaching the Bb in measure 3. Each example articulates different chord tones, yet they all strongly emphasize the downbeat of measure three. As the BbMaj7 in measure 3 is a cadence, our ear will listen for that arrival more than a chord like the Gm7. Variation 1 articulates scale degrees 5-4-3-2-1 in the key of Bb, providing a very strong cadence, even if it doesn't necessarily outline all of the chord tones vertically.

If we continue with the same Bb Major Bebop scale in measures 5-8, the scale would not articulate any chord tones which isn't useful. In order to continue the descending scale shape we'll need to use the Eb Major Bebop scale. Why? In measures 5-6 there is a Bb7 followed by an EbMaj7, functioning as a V-I cadence in the key of Eb Major. This means that for two bars, *we are temporarily in Eb Major*. The Eb Major Bebop scale accounts for the change in tonality and still leads strongly back to the BbMaj7 in measure 7. Example 4.6 begins on the 5th scale degree to match up with the Bb7—look at how well it articulates the harmony:

Example 4.6

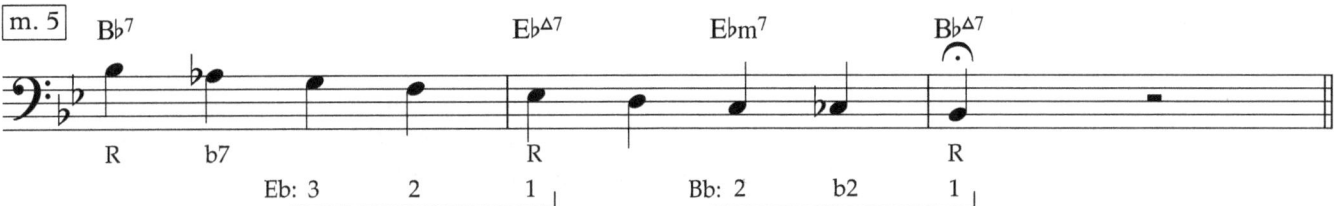

Beginning in measure 5, we can also ascend the Bb Dominant Bebop scale starting on the 5th to address the harmony. Whenever you see a dominant chord without a preceding ii7 chord, you can always add a ii7 chord without disrupting the harmony (and conversely, you can ignore the ii7 too and only play the V7 chord). In measure 5 of rhythm changes you can outline a ii-V to IV, which is what using the following scale does anyway:

Example 4.7

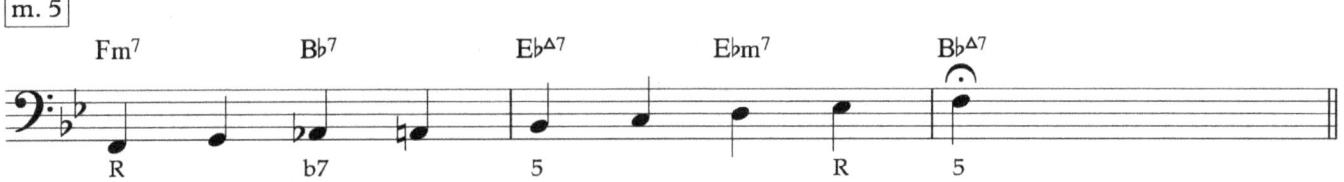

In measures 1-5, you can even start descending and change to ascending halfway through:

Example 4.8

There are many ways in which the Bebop scales can be used to walk bass lines, and I encourage you to explore this idea further on your own. Use my way of thinking about chord/scale relationships to find what sounds good to your ear.

The bridge:

The bridge is a great place to walk using the Dominant Bebop scale. You can still vary the starting notes so it's not always the root, but I've found starting this scale with the root (and sometimes 5th which will be demonstrated) makes for the most convincing line both vertically and linearly. Phrase your lines in two or four bar segments, meaning when you get to the II7 chord (5th bar of the bridge) start with a new scale or change direction.

As a reminder, the bridge changes are **III7** - **VI7** - **II7** - **V7**. While the bridge temporarily moves to a different key center, the key signature remains the same. Lets demonstrate the first four bars of the bridge, descending the Dominant Bebop scale:

Example 4.9

We reach our target note, D, on beat 1. This creates a **delayed root resolution** with two simple solutions to finishing the line. G can be approached on the downbeat of the fourth measure using scale degrees 5-4-3-2-1 (similar to Method 3's WS-WS-R approach in major) to reach your cadence. Continuing to descend the bebop scale can also work, but, in order to continue the scale and still reach our target a note will have to be added. If you were to continue walking the scale without any adjustment, G would occur on beat 2.

Example 4.10 uses the Dominant Bebop scale with a 5-4-3-2-1 approach to G7. Scale degrees 5-4-3-2-1 function in the key of G.

🎧 **Example 4.10**

Example 4.11 uses an extra note in measure three to ensure a resolution on the downbeat of measure four.

🎧 **Example 4.11**

In order for the line to resolve strongly on the downbeat of measure 4, I used D on beat 4, allowing for a resolution on the downbeat. Had I continued the scale, A would have been articulated on the downbeat. By using D on beat 4, it emphasizes the C natural on beat 3, creating greater tension in the walking line. The 7th of D7 (C) voice leads to the 3rd of G7 (B), and I resolve that particular tension on beat 1 of measure 4 before continuing my line. Notice how scale degrees 5-4-3 in G are effectively outlined.

Being aware of how 3rds and 7ths resolve within a walking line helps you keep track of all the possible harmonic target points. If we continued the line without any manipulation, we wouldn't be able to play a chord tone on the downbeat of G7. By adding the extra note, I was able to adequately reach the resolution point. This is what target points are all about: aiming for a note and figuring out how to accurately arrive there while making adjustments along the way. This is why the Bebop scale works so well in this context—it's an introduction to controlled chromaticism that can help add variety to your arrivals without much effort.

If you start on the 5th of the D Dominant Bebop scale and descend, you can accomplish the exact same resolution as the previous example, just one bar earlier:

🎧 **Example 4.12**

The reason we still resolve to B on the downbeat of the G7 chord is the 7th (in D7) will be left unresolved—the ear still hears this hanging note, so, we must add one more note to properly voice lead our line. You can use a variety of passing tones to accomplish this; just make sure all your thirds and sevenths are accounted for. We make our resolution on beat two.

As the bridge is sequential, you can do a literal transposition of these ideas starting on C7 and they will be equally as effective.

Other thoughts on rhythm changes...

This is just a starting point. These scales provide a systematic way to start formulating longer lines with consistency and are not the only way to approach rhythm changes. Food for thought:

1) When you reach a new chord, continue the same line shape but switch scales.
2) You're allowed to break up the scale (such as the extra non-scalar tone above).
3) The best bass lines are a combination of many walking techniques.

On the next page is a final example culminating all the techniques in one chorus of rhythm changes:

Example 4.13

Bb Rhythm Changes

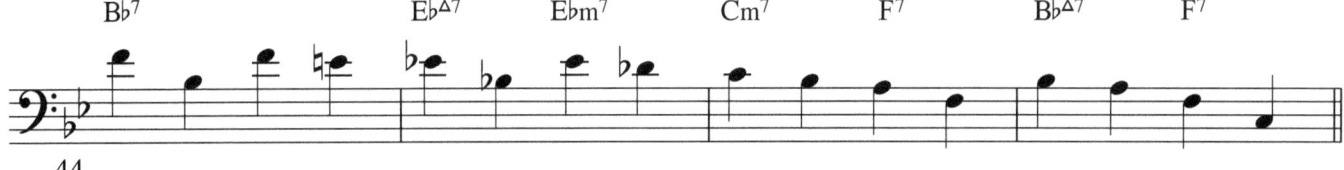

Points to consider in practice and playing with others

- Play these lines on your bass. When working on the bridge, your lines will be dictated by how you comfortably navigate through the bass. If you've been practicing your diatonic arpeggios and chords, you'll find yourself able to play longer lines due to an increased understanding of the fingerboard.

- There will be trial and error before you figure out what bebop scales you can use. It'll be some time before you can switch instinctively between scales. Knowing what key you're headed to will help you learn what's appropriate.

- Start picking target notes in your lines and see what scale paths reach that specific target.

- Experiment—first and foremost, aim for clarity in your lines.

- Practice these in 12 keys and see what transpositions work better than others. A line in C Major won't be played the same in B Major due to the layout shifting and a lack of open strings. Having specific key-specific walking vocabulary is totally okay—every bass player does.

Chapter 5
Modal Tunes

Our study of modal tunes will add more depth to the idea of targeted arrival points in lines. This chapter will continue our discussion of scales, and lead to creating your own scale sounds using triad pairs. Triad pairs can be effective when sequencing melodic cells, helping to add more variety to your lines.

In brief, modal jazz refers to a way of conceptualizing progressions that is based around scales rather than chord changes. Typically, modal tunes allow players to spend significant time in a single mode before moving to a new collection of notes. This represents a sort of opposite to the rhythm changes described in Chapter 4: rather than changing chords every two measures, some modal tunes are constructed to let performers play with the same scale for as much as 16 measures at a time. **Mode** is sort of a fancy synonym for scale. Another name for the major scale is the Ionian mode. By keeping the same collection of notes but choosing a new "home" pitch or starting note for a scale, you can explore other modes. For example, if you keep the same pitches that are in the C Ionian mode (C major scale) but start and end your scale on D, you will be playing the D Dorian mode.

Many modal tunes are commonly minor based, so our bass lines in this chapter will be based off of the changes from "So What." "So What" is from the 1959 Miles Davis album *Kind of Blue*, one of the quintessential jazz albums. The method used to create scales and lines in minor modal keys can easily be applied to major modal sounds too. Tunes like "So What" are known for the openness of the harmony, containing long stretches of the same sound palate. While the tune is written in the Dorian mode, the only soloist on the recording that most strictly adheres to this mode is Miles Davis. Cannonball Adderley and John Coltrane both explore different types of minor sounds (harmonic, melodic, etc) in their solos, with Bill Evans adapting accordingly in his comping.

How do we walk over such an open tune with so many possibilities?

The first thing to consider is the key and the possible minor sounds. Here are four minor scales using D as the root:

Example 5.1

These are all different flavors of minor with alterations to the 6th and the 7th scale degrees. Any of these minor sounds can be used in your walking lines. With these long stretches of the same sound, you can take liberties including exploring new (related) scales. Methods 1 and 2 still apply here, too.

Here's an 8 bar example based on the changes of "So What" that mixes the Dorian and Melodic Minor scales:

🎧 **Example 5.2**

In this example, most of the bass line stays in Dorian. Measure 4 uses C# from A7 and Melodic Minor in measure 8 as a way to cadence (mark the form) every four measures. The C# is the leading tone in D Minor, regardless of mode, and is a musical/aural sign that keeps the phrase lengths evenly organized. There are three strategies I use to form this line:

1) Scalar shapes (measures 1-2)
2) Sequencing intervallic leaps (measure 3 and measures 5-6)
3) Tonicization of the home key (measures 4/8)

One of my favorite strategies is number 2: sequencing melodic fragments through the mode. Because of the arrangement of notes in the mode, the sequence will eventually incorporate the interesting notes (in this case natural 6) and add more color to your line. This is also called planing—taking an idea and sequencing it diatonically (ascending or descending) without any changes to the content or intervals. Bill Evans effectively planes chordal sounds when comping on "So What."

How else can we create more variety in our bass lines?

Through the use of **Triad Pairs**. One of my favorite line-creating concepts is borrowed from guitarists and pianists. Sequencing two triads that are derived from a mode is a way to add depth and more harmonic possibilities in your line. Visit page 18 for a refresher on triad pairs.

1) Begin with choosing a mode. In the case of "So What," it's D Dorian.

2) Pick two triads that don't share any notes, avoiding pairs that area 3rd or 5th apart, such as CMaj and Emin. Your choices include:

CMaj Dmin Emin FMaj GMaj Amin Bm7b5

3) Arpeggiate your first chord, only three notes, and then arpeggiate your second chord. After completing this in root position, arpeggiate your first chord again, this time starting on the chordal 3rd. For example, if you played C-E-G first, this time you'll play E-G-C.

4) Continue arpeggiating all the chords until you've successfully done it for one octave.

Example 5.3 demonstrates the sequencing of a Dmin and CMaj triad pair. In doing this, you essentially create a harmonized six-note scale. Again, you can create your own scale sounds by picking two different triads from whatever mode you're in. Scale degree 6 is missing from this example, but I could have used Emin in place of CMaj if I wanted to articulate the 6th. Randomly picked triads, such as EbMaj and Bmin, will not work in this application. In order for this idea to work, the triads *must be derived from mode you're in.*

Example 5.3

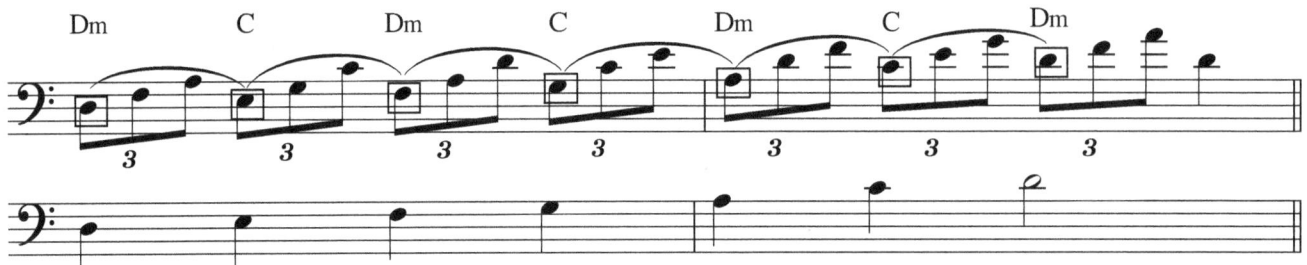

Now when choosing a note for your walking line, you'll have an understanding of how that note is harmonized and what other options you may have harmonically. Example 5.4 demonstrates sequencing Dmin and Emin triad sounds in measures 5-6.

Example 5.4

Knowing where these triads are positioned on the bass gives you better access to potential melodic material. From any fixed note, you should be able to play almost any interval. So really, the limit is your imagination.

One final note: in "So What," Paul Chambers sometimes walked the Dm7 sections with G in the bass and the Ebm7 sections with Ab in the bass. This changes the color of the harmony without changing the function of the chord. You cannot change root notes willy-nilly, but, in this case of this particular modal tone, moving the root of Dm7 up a fourth to G won't destabilize the harmony. I've demonstrated this in measure 29 of "So What."

With that said, here's one chorus example based on the changes "So What" that uses a combination of all of these concepts:

Example 5.5

So What

Watch for the use of:

1) Melodic Minor
2) Melodic sequencing of triad pairs in the bridge
3) G as the root in measure 29

Points to consider in practice and playing with others

- Continue phrasing your bass lines in bigger pieces, starting with two measures and working up to four- and eight-bar phrases. Scales can help this by getting you to your destination with a predetermined sequence of notes.

- When creating target notes in your line, think about all the available notes (from whatever position you're in) above and below the note you're playing at that moment. This helps to fill in the fingerboard visually, keep track of all the possibilities, and prevent you from losing your place on the instrument.

- Playing these sounds on the piano really helps to show the different colors and reinforce the last bullet point—you'll hear which sounds you like better than others. Learning to voice simple chords on piano is extremely useful for this.

- Transcribe both Paul Chambers and Ron Carter walking on "So What"; it'll give you great insight to how they walk over modal tunes.

Chapter 6
Constructing Advanced Linear Bass Lines

With your understanding of counterpoint and bass lines deepening, you'll soon recognize that not all functional and successful bass lines adhere to the patterns from this book. These formulas represent common patterns that bassists use and will create completely functional lines. However, they're not the end point—they merely serve as the point of departure for you to create sounds and patterns for your own walking vocabulary. My biggest influence when I began playing was Ray Brown. I love his sound and feel, but I especially love the melodic nature of his walking lines. What was so melodic about them? He had clear destinations, nothing went unresolved and he was always playing with a purpose. *He was always taking the music somewhere.* The purpose of this chapter is to venture deeper into the idea of linear target points for the purpose of helping you to develop your own concepts.

A bass line's harmonic goal is to delineate chords vertically while also expressing a line in a forward-moving direction, that is, to a projection point: harmonic cadence, pillars of the form, key changes, etc. By now this should be understood conceptually. How do you advance your understanding, though? Most importantly, **how do you know what's right or not?** To start, you should feel generally comfortable with the harmony of the tune you're playing. Beyond just the chord changes, this includes: identifying ii-V-I progressions, key centers, cadences, etc. All of these become easier to identify and hear with more playing experience.

Let's refer to "Autumn Leaves" as an example. There are two key areas: Bb Major and G Minor. The person calling the tune will identify the key before playing, or, you can look at the key signature of the lead sheet to see how many flats/sharps there are. Beyond that, identifying the key centers within a tune can be done by looking for a V7-I resolution. In "Autumn Leaves," one example would be F7-BbMaj7. In measures 1-4, Cm7-F7-BbMaj7, we are in the key of Bb Major. In the measures containing Am7b5-D7-Gm, we are in G Minor. Again, I looked for a V7-I (or i) resolution and saw D7-Gmin. Train yourself to identify these when reading lead sheets. Eventually, this will become second nature.

For this chapter, we will generally follow two rules: our target points will be minor or major cadences (again, characterized by V7-I or V7-i motion), and our target points will group our bass lines into two or four-measure chunks.

A solid bassist will pair good note choice with rhythmic activity (coming later) to outline the song form in their lines and lead the band. In a way, they are the architects of the music. In this chapter, arrival points will be approached using the chromatic scale to strengthen your understanding. Where do we start?

The blues

The blues is an easy way to start practicing advanced linear constructions.

1) Choose a key (in this case, F) and start your line on the root of the I chord.
2) Pick a harmonically stable arrival point in F7, 2-4 measures away.
   - Harmonically, this can be a root, 3rd, or 5th—any type of consonant sound in F7
   - Rhythmically, the downbeat of measure 3 works well as it's a IV-I cadence (albeit not as strong as V-I). The effect of resolving here would be stronger than, say, beat three of the same measure.
3) Pick a direction (generally it's easiest to start descending).
4) Aim for chord tones like 1,3,5,b7 on strong beats (1 and 3) and place your weaker, less consonant notes on weak beats (2 and 4).
   - Using non-harmonic tones on weak beats helps connect strong chord tones.
   - Enclosures (surrounding a consonance) are effective

Example 6.1

We have two goals here: outline vertical harmony in our walking line, and also keep the line moving towards a direction/target. We still need to play the chord tones, but if your target point is strong, ultimately the linear projection of your bass line trumps the vertical information. That's not to say we can take Bb7 and play it as a Min7, or, completely ignore the chord qualities in general. If you come to a point where you may need to play a "wrong" note but it eventually hits a strong resolution, that's okay. Example 6.2 provides two solutions to example 6.1:

Example 6.2

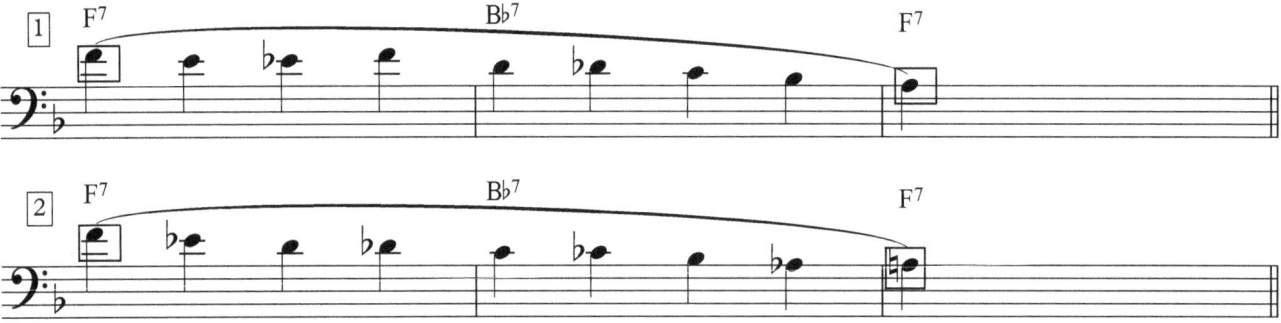

- Variation 1 is straight-forward. Measure two starts on the chordal 3rd and walks down to A. Looking back from measure 3, the line can be justified because every sequential note clearly leads to A.
- Variation 2 is more chromatic, and vertically makes less sense than variation 1. The closer we get to our arrival point, we lead in a way that will emphasize the A. This results in a bigger release of harmonic tension. The resolution to the root of the chord in measure two happens on beat 3, serving as the first of two pitches that enclose the 3rd of F7 from above and below. So while it may be hard to sell this line vertically, the line is given context when it lands convincingly on the third of the tonic. Lines like this can be very useful in creating stronger tension and release.

Here's one of my favorite examples of a long bass line over "Freddie Freeloader." This line features Ray Brown from the album *Live at Scullers*:

Example 6.3

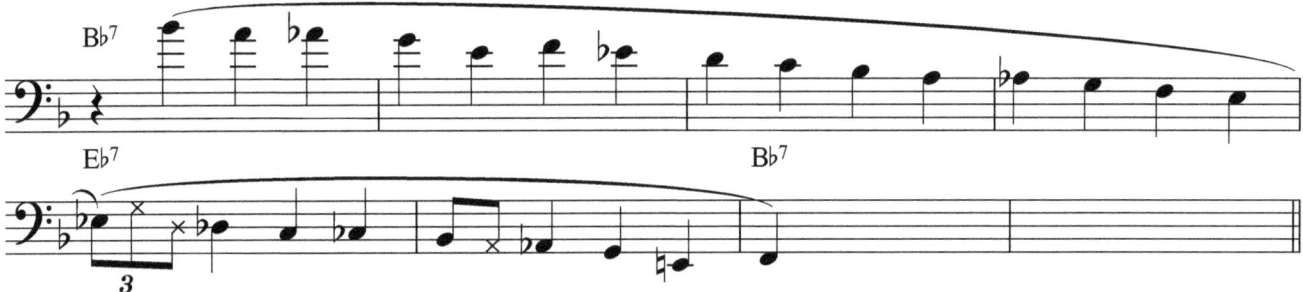

Things to notice about this line:
- The line begins on beat 2—this is an effect used by bass players to create tension at the beginning of a new section, when transitioning from a two-feel to walking, etc. Only use it at the very beginning of your line.
- Starting in measure 2, Ray phrases his line with a pattern of chord tones on strong beats (1 and 3) and passing tones on weak beats (2 and 4).
- While the line articulates the root of the Eb7 in measure 5, the final arrival occurs with the return of Bb7 in measure 7, which Brown approaches by enclosing the F.
- Primary (F) and secondary (Eb) arrival points marked by slur
- This line covers the whole range of the bass—the effect of a line with this much range is huge! This gives the arrival point greater emphasis.

This Ray Brown line gives us more insight to the purpose of linear lines:

1) The linear direction of moving from point A ——> B will trump what's happening vertically if the destination point is strong. In example 7.2, measure 2, I begin on the chordal third and don't articulate Bb until beat four. Isolating only 2 two looks strange, but in context it works just fine.
2) Lines with longer destination points offer the chance to be more melodic and sequence material.
3) Use of range in bass lines can be the most powerful tool in our arsenal. For example, starting in the upper register at the beginning of a solo can make the groove lighter—a gradual descent into the low register (aiming for the arrival) before eventually stabilizing into a groove can create a burst of energy in the band.
4) Because these lines are destination oriented, they're effective at anticipating arrivals to new keys. Method 4 (R CT WS WS) gives insight to this as it is effectively 3-2-1 in the new key, two beats before it arrives. Linear construction can help us anticipate this even earlier, marking a more absolute transition into the new key center.
5) Lines happen in every direction. While most of my examples are descending, line ascension creates an equally effective mood.

Just to show how far this idea can be taken, here's a 12 bar blues in F:

Example 6.4

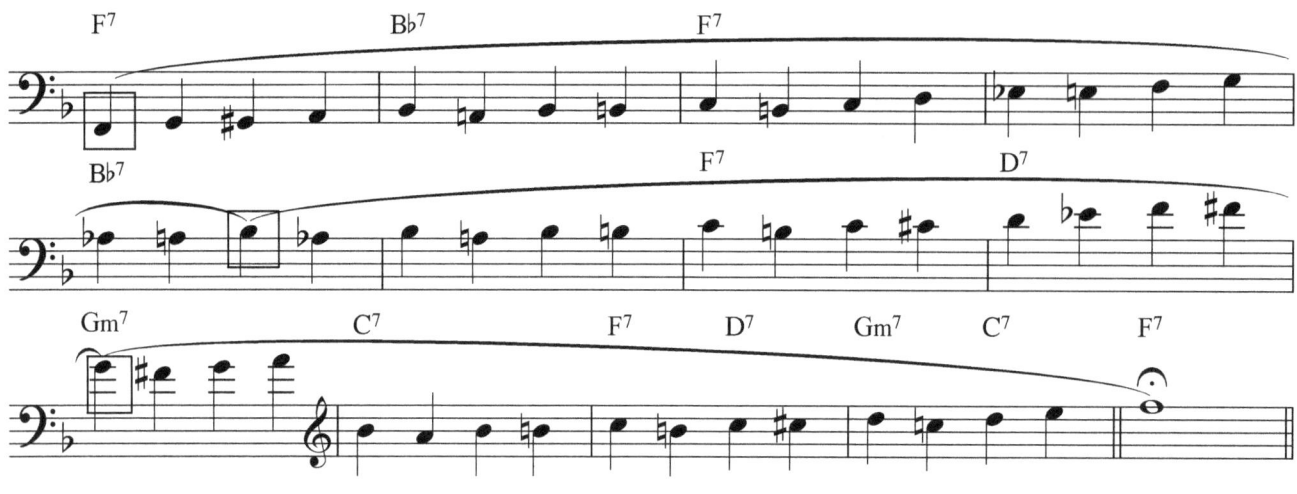

This is a 12 measure line with a final arrival point of F, three octaves above the starting root. There are two secondary arrivals, in measures 5 and 9, before the final cadence point. Notice the use of chromaticism and neighboring tones on weak beats to help strengthen the final arrival point. How you decide to phrase these is up to your own artistic discretion. I still manage to target mostly root notes, and despite what's happening vertically the linear points are still clear. Just to be clear, linear bass lines do *not* have to be only ascending or only descending—linear bass lines can move in both directions. In this context, linear means aiming for a targeted note that you approach stepwise (without wide intervallic leaps).

Standards

We've seen this work over the blues, so let's look at examples over standards and a John Coltrane tune. See what you can identify in these written examples. Example 6.5 is based on the changes of "East of the Sun" by Brooks Bowman.

Example 6.5

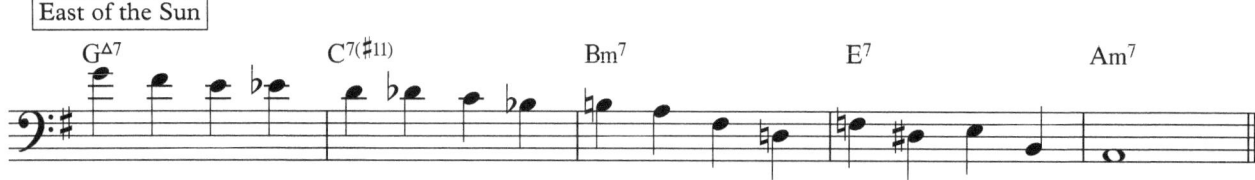

The line begins chromatically (Bebop Scale), adding further chromaticism after D to delay arriving to the C, before arriving at the targeted Bm7. Beats 3 and 4 of measure 2 act as an enclosure to the B—this choice was made to prevent B from being articulated on beat four of measure 3. Another enclosure happens around E before cadencing in A minor.

Example 6.6 is based off of the changes of "Isfahan" by Duke Ellington. The use of doubled notes allows us to pace the arrival point more slowly, increasing activity as we approach our final destination.

🎧 **Example 6.6**

Example 6.7 is based on Herbie Hancock's changes to "You're My Everything" (from Freddie Hubbard's *Hub-Tones*) by Mort Dixon, Joe Young and Harry Warren. I chose to ascend here, hitting different target points than I normally would, particularly in measure 3. The line has a different aesthetic but reaches the target just the same.

🎧 **Example 6.7**

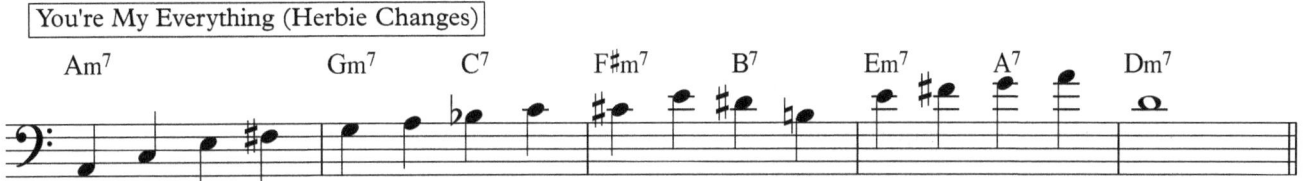

Example 6.8 is based off of the changes to "Giant Steps" by John Coltrane. It forgoes vertical harmony in favor of a linear direction. I use 3-2-1 as my arrival into Eb instead of explicitly articulating Bb7. This is a smooth way to lead the ear into new keys. A marker of "Giant Steps" is quickly moving key centers around a Major 3rds cycle.

🎧 **Example 6.8**

… Of course, your path to creating linear bass lines is personal and will be influenced by who you listen to, what level of theory knowledge you have, etc. Having your basic seventh chords and major/minor scales will be more than enough to prepare you for constructing these types of lines. All of these examples lead to the final method for practicing linear constructions.

How can we best practice target points? With the **Chromatic Scale.**

Using the chromatic scale to anticipate arrival points

Bassists develop the ability to anticipate target notes from a distance away. Are there 8 notes until my resolution? 7? 12? After playing for a while, it's not consciously thought of—it's heard and felt. Practicing using the chromatic scale is a way to help develop that intuitive sense:

1) Set the metronome to 60bpm, with each pulse indicating a quarter note.
2) Pick a key for the Blues—F or Bb work well to start.
3) Pick a low or high octave for the root of the first chord and a direction. A high root should descend and a low root should ascend. Give yourself enough range to work with.
   - Give yourself enough range to work with—descending from C on the A string, for example, will severely limit your line.
4) Play the chromatic scale in quarter notes over a two-octave span.
5) Change directions and play the chromatic scale until you reach the root again. This direction change should occur at the exact half point, beat 1 of measure 7. On the downbeat of the second chorus the root should be re-articulated.
   - Pay attention to the chord tones or resolutions that naturally occur when walking. How many chromatic notes precede the resolution? Are there any sequences of notes that mark form successfully? What do you like?

Most important is to pay attention to what chord tones and resolutions line up in measures that make sense. Example 6.9 demonstrates using an F Blues:

Example 6.9

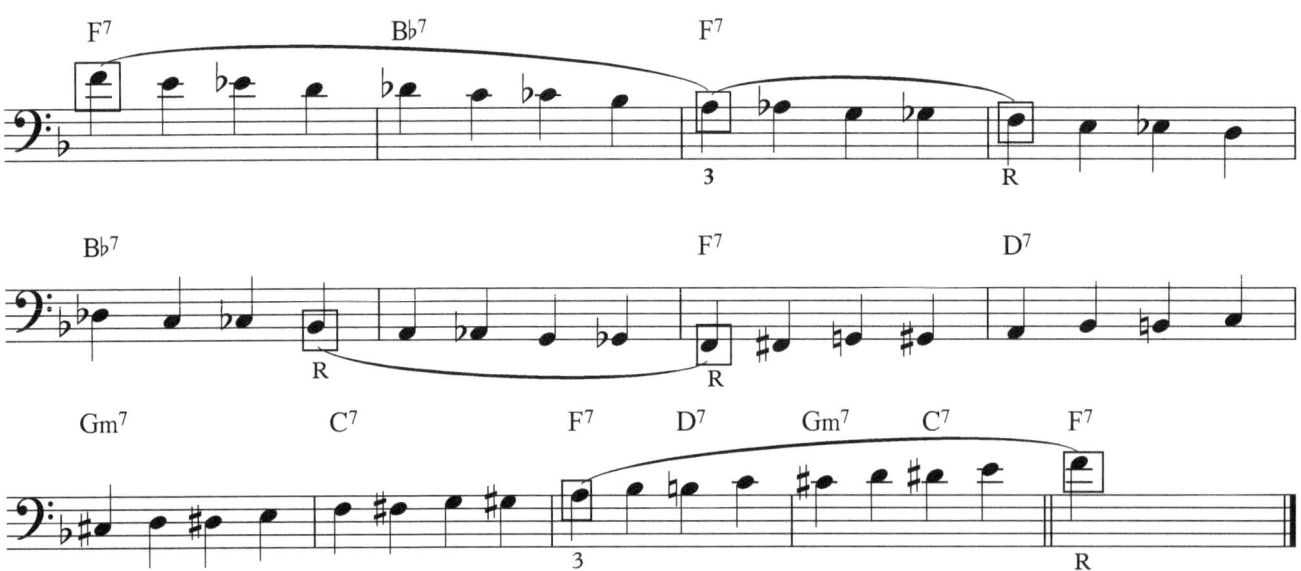

I've highlighted three options from Example 6.9 I believe make usable resolutions and target points.

1) The first marked example is a 13-note line with a final resolution to the root in measure 4 and a secondary arrival point (A on F7). You could use this bit of material, break away from the chromatic scale and resolve to Bb on the downbeat of measure 5.

2) The second example is not as compelling, as it places A natural on the strong beat of a Bb7 chord, but since Bb is played before it and is followed by strong chromaticism to the root, the arrival to F is still felt.

3) The third example is similar to example one but instead ascends. Around the C#, your ear recognizes that F will be resolved to on the downbeat and creates a convincing resolution in your bass line.

Starting on the root when practicing these exercises is the easiest way to conceptualize them. If you'd like to experiment with different arrivals, begin on the 5th of your tonic chord. I've highlighted a few workable arrival points. Depending on the key you may need to move your line up the octave in order to maintain direction.

Example 6.10

The targets in Example 6.10 arrive on 7ths and 5ths. Measure 3 begins on the Major 7th instead of flatted 7th—that can be okay! Because the resolution is strong, it justifies what happens before it. Major 7ths can be used (very) sparingly on dominants—Tommy Flanagan's solo on the blues "Big Paul," from *Kenny Burrell & John Coltrane*, makes use of the Major 7 on a dominant chord. Doug Watkins on "KB Blues" articulates a Major 7th on the downbeat of a dominant chord in his walking line. Many recordings have usage of Major 7ths on dominant chords. They can't all be interchanged freely, but, in situations where they naturally occur in a linear direction it's okay.

Let's examine target notes on a standard. We'll create two examples, both based on the changes from the first four bars of "Autumn Leaves." The first one will descend chromatically from C and the second one will ascend from C.

Example 6.11

There is not a lot of outright usable musical material in these examples. *This will take some creative thinking on your part to make it work.* These are exercises to help you recognize arrival points. Not every instance will be the best and most musical choice. You should move away from the chromatic scale when you realize you may need to manipulate a few notes in order to make a successful resolution.

Lets take the first 7 notes of the scale and make F on the BbMaj7 chord our target:

🎧 **Example 6.12**

I saw potential for a resolution on the fifth of BbMaj7, so I treated the Gb as an opportunity for an enclosure around the F by using E as well. This gave me time to properly prepare the resolution. Resolve to Bb on beat 2 and you're good to go.

In Example 6.13, we're still guided by the chromatic scale, only this time we're going to start it in the middle of the phrase. This provides an opportunity for a nice melodic sequence in measures 3 and 4:

🎧 **Example 6.13**

The chromatic line aims for a delayed root of the chord in measure 4, and the b7 on the downbeat provides stronger tension. When you sequence the Bb7 pattern over the EbMaj7 chord it strengthens the melodic content of the line. This definitely requires a bit of thinking outside of the box, but it shows how opportunities for chromaticism and melodic sequencing are almost everywhere.

You can apply this concept in the middle of a line—almost anywhere that has a potential target note is fair game. Example 6.14 uses the changes of "East of the Sun" as an example. Descending chromatically from the root will still lead us smoothly to the Bmin7. Just like in the earlier methods, the root does not always need to land on the downbeat, especially in passing chords. This flexibility allows more options for chromatic lines.

🎧 **Example 6.14**

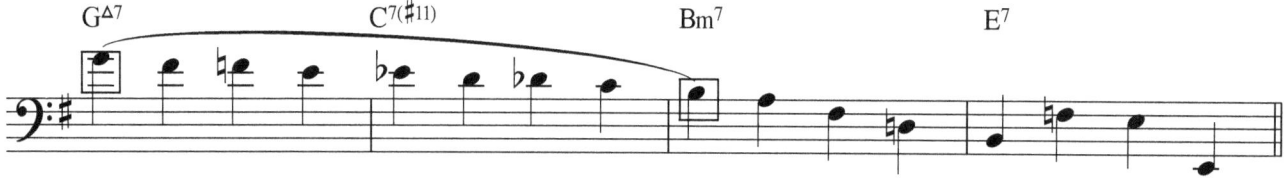

What if we start descending chromatically from the Bmin7 instead?

🎧 Example 6.15

The second example leads well to Amin7, with a b9-8 motion strengthening the cadence. Both clearly project target notes/resolutions that make sense to the ear. Just one more example to demonstrate how you can utilize chromaticism. The only limit is your imagination.

On the following page, you'll find Example 6.16, a full chorus based off the changes of "East of the Sun." It ties together *all* of the methods used throughout the book so far. I analyze the target points and chromatic arrivals. In some instances, I started on the 9th of Min7 chords for smooth voice leading. See what other methods and devices you can pick up on.

Points to consider in practice and playing with others

- Study lines by as many bassists as you can—Israel Crosby, Paul Chambers, Wilbur Ware, Ray Brown, Rufus Reid, Sam Jones, Jimmy Blanton, Ron Carter, and Doug Watkins, just to name a few. Each bassist handles the role of the bass with variety and equal success.
- Learn bebop melodies on the bass. Donna Lee is great as it contains many target points that are approached chromatically *and* easy to visualize. Learning bebop melodies helps to strengthen your layout and gives you additional material to use. Again, strive to know the melodies to all of tunes you play.
- These ideas are meant to serve as exercises. Is a chromatic scale the most melodic sound to play? Maybe, maybe not. It can certainly help unlock what you consider to be an appropriate thread to connect your chosen target points.
- Always think about where your line is going. Time doesn't happen vertically and neither does a bass line—it's only contextualized by where it's headed to. Where are you taking the music in your line? What purpose does the line serve? Uncontrolled chromaticism for the sake of a "hip" line can be to the detriment of the music. Always be thinking: "How am I serving the music?"
- Sequence melodic ideas chromatically to add relevant variety in your lines. Strive to make your bass the most melodic element of what's happening in any band.
- *LISTEN*. Often times, my ideas are fueled by taking fragments of what someone else has played and using that to create my own melodic material. It happens vice versa and strengthens the dialogue in the band—communication definitely happens in two directions.
- Explore these lines in places that are not as comfortable on the bass to you. Don't settle for being mostly comfortable with your instrument—know where you are.
- *GO FOR IT!* If your idea doesn't pan out as planned but you still have a clear target, finish anyways and go for it the second chorus around. Reuse of material is expected. Practice line ideas while supporting a band and you'll get a quick sense of how musical your ideas are.

Example 6.16

East of the Sun

Example 6.17

East of the Sun

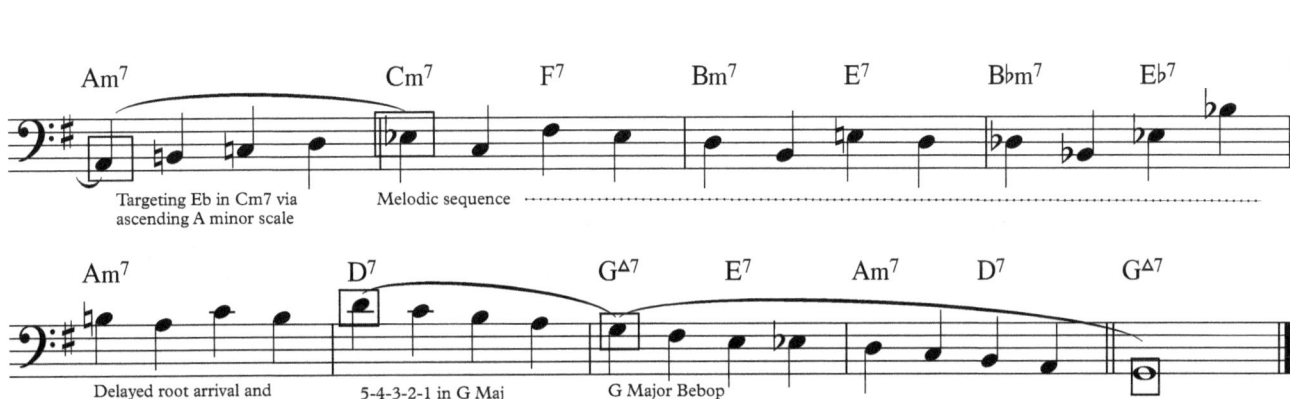

Chapter 7
The Two Feel

While the purpose of this book is to talk about four beat line, mention should be made of how a (very) basic two feel works. There are many ways to approach a two feel. Traditionally the origins of the two-beat feel are rooted in dance music. In a jazz setting, it provides a grounded groove that can "sit" for a while; it has less forward motion than a walking feel and provides more of a bounce. You can build up energy and release when the band kicks into a four feel. One of my favorite bassists for a two feel is Israel Crosby from the Ahmad Jamal Trio. Without getting too in-depth (as it could be a Pandora's box of all sorts of styles) here are a few basics thoughts for establishing a functional two feel.

1) Familiarize yourself with bassists' two feels. Some of my favorites include Israel Crosby, Sam Jones, Ray Brown, Wilbur Ware, Paul Chambers, Christian McBride and George Morrow. This is by no means an all-inclusive list!

2) To start, don't play too complicated. A two-beat feel is exactly what the name implies—two beats per measure, with just a kick of rhythmic activity in the right place. I strive to make it bouncy and dance-able. They largely follow four bar phrases (over standards), with a bit more activity at the end of the phrase to increase the forward motion towards phrase endings.

3) Experiment with note length. Is your two-beat feel a literal half note with no space in between the notes? A long quarter note with a slight space in between? Do you release your left hand directly on the downbeat? Your note lengths can drastically affect how the groove is felt by the band. For the purpose of this book, any time you read a two-beat feel it'll be written in half-notes. It's up to you to interpret the subtleties in the groove. Some bass players like to play long-sustained half notes in their two feels, with others leaving a marked space in between (almost like a dotted quarter note and eighth rest). How will you do it?

Here's an example of a very basic two feel, based on the changes of "All of Me."

🎧Example 7.1

Notice two things about this line:

1) It contains mostly roots and 5ths. You don't need to embellish much harmonically. As you're the fundamental supporting role, you shouldn't be concerned with doing too much filler material.

2) The rhythmic activity picks up before a cadence or arrival point. More activity usually means more motion (think about two-beat vs four beat), and timing this towards the ends of phrases delivers the music there more effectively.

If you'd like to do something a bit more melodic, follow a guide tone line. Remember example 6.16 of "Isfahan" from the previous chapter with the doubled notes? If you have a strong projection point in mind, let that lead you. Here's what "Isfahan" looks like if you take the same walking line and transform it into a two feel:

🎧 **Example 7.2**

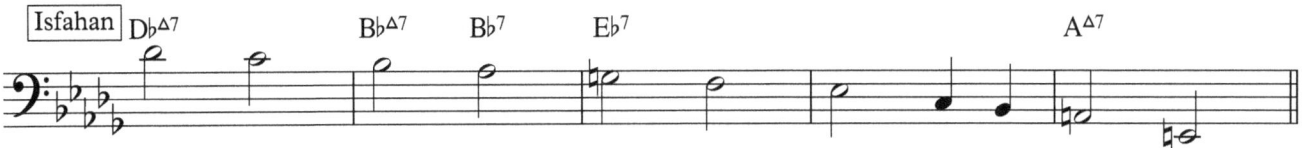

This method for conceptualizing two feels will work over many of the standards tunes you'll encounter. Adjustments need to be made for playing in 3 (a "one feel"). For one example of varying the rhythm in a two feel, check out Ron Carter's bass playing with Jim Hall, and Miles' Second Quintet.

Points to consider in practice and playing with others

- Listen to early dance music (1920's and 30's) and a variety of rhythm sections to give yourself a good idea of how a two-beat has evolved over time. Take notice of note length, articulation, and overall how it changes the momentum of the music.

- Try playing a two-beat feel with the bow for a New Orleans tuba-style groove. How does this change the way the music feels?

- There are as many variations of two feels as there are walking lines. Up to this point, you have probably been focusing primarily on walking lines in recordings. There will certainly be two-feels on many of the recordings you're already checking out. Shift your focus to the two-feels and try to listen for variations in content similarly to how you do with walking lines.

- Subdivide when you're playing. If you focus on the big beat (1&3) when you're playing, the time might feel too stationery—subdivide four beats internally so your feel doesn't stagnate.

Chapter 8
Adding Rhythmic Material to Your Lines

I purposely chose to put this section in last. Why? Because rhythmic material is the icing on the cake. Fundamental understanding of how proper lines are created is necessary before trying to embellish them. Rhythmic activity will make a great line better and a bad line worse. It's much too easy to overdo activity in a line and ruin the function. A contrapuntally strong line stands on its own and doesn't need much else to make it sound good. One properly placed drop or 8th note skip can do more for the music than a few poorly placed triplets.

Just as in harmonic choices, each bassist's rhythmic activity is highly personalized. Some bassists such as Ray Brown, Sam Jones, and Ron Carter have more activity in their lines. Other bassists, like Paul Chambers or Curly Russell, use quarter notes to propel their lines. One approach is no more effective than the other.

The most common rhythms to incorporate in your bass lines are 8th notes (swung) and triplets. Ray Brown commonly utilized triplets and variations of in his bass playing, with an effect coined as "hick-it-y boom." (Note: there is no official way to spell this effect). It provides extra momentum for the band with a big release of energy. Hitting low E hard at the end of this is an effect that should be used *sparingly*.

I always think of drums to help me conceptualize rhythmic activity. The swing beat, played on the ride cymbal, is a series of alternating quarter notes and swung eighth notes. The swung 8ths are known as the skip beat since they break the quarter note pattern (and you skip the second partial of the triplet). Bass lines can also contain skip beats.

You can use **swung eighth notes** in place of any of the quarter notes in a measure. Lets take a two measure phrase and place a different set of eight notes on each beat:

Example 8.1

Eighth notes can occur on any beat in the measure. There are general places in the form you'll want to use these rhythmic fillers: in the beginning of a phrase (new A section, top of the form, etc), towards the end of a phrase, and in transition points. Placing eighth notes is effective at the very beginning of a line to give an initial "burst' of energy. Eighth notes can also be effective in the middle of a walking phrase to keep the momentum going. You'll want to vary where you place these in your line so you're not stuck playing the same rhythmic material—it'll get boring quick.

Here are variations on the eighth note fill:

Example 8.2

I've noticed Ray Brown use the first variation often, and Sam Jones/Doug Watkins commonly using the second variation. One has the extra eighth note "hiccup" in there. Both examples vary the rhythmic drive; use them at your discretion. Again, you can place the eighth notes or tied eighth notes on any beat. Just don't overdo it.

The other option for rhythmic activity is **triplets**. Triplets commonly happen with dead (muted) notes noted as an "x." This is an effective technique in creating a burst of energy right from the get-go. Notes in triplets usually descend high to low. The addition of rhythmic energy plus the descent in range makes for a strong effect. Christian McBride uses strings of triplets in a row (sometimes two or three) to really pick up the energy. Again, appropriate timing is key to making this musical.

If a triplet contains any muted notes, the first note is commonly sounded, followed by a muted note on that same string, a muted note on the string below, and then your target note. You make these notes "dead" by half-pushing down your left hand against the string; not enough to engage a sound but still making contact. You can use open strings if you're playing over a chord that contains one or more of those sounds (F Major, C Major, D Major, G Major, etc).

You don't have to play all three partials of triplets. Measure three of Example 8.3 has a rest on the first partial of the triplet which is another common phrase of bass vocabulary. Measure four shows an extreme high to low, exaggerating just how much distance you can get out of these rhythmic drops. You can use these on any beats:

Example 8.3

Between the combinations of eighth notes and triplets, there's more than enough rhythmic material to incorporate into your lines. Think about all the places you can apply different skip beats and see what works most effectively.

Example 8.4 on the next page shows how I'd add rhythmic activity to a tune based off of the changes of "East of The Sun." I admit that this transcription looks busy—look where I place activity and sequences and use it to inspire your own creativity. Ultimately you should listen to the recording to hear how I phrase my eighth notes and accents—not all have the same velocity.

Example 8.4 — East of the Sun

Points to consider in practice and playing with others

- The best way to learn rhythmic vocabulary is by listening to recordings. Each bassist has their own variation on adding rhythmic activity to their lines, so find a bassist that appeals to you and learn how they incorporate their vocabulary.

- If a full melodic dictation is too daunting, do rhythmic transcriptions of walking bass lines. Write down the rhythmic information and notice where they place fills. Try making your own bass line using these same rhythmic patterns.

- Use sparingly until you feel you can confidently add it. The easiest way to ruin a line is add too many skip beats and busy moments. One properly placed rhythmic addition is much more effective than a lot for the sake of doing something hip!

- If you're walking a line and realize you may need to add/subtract a note to meet your target point, adding rhythmic activity can effectively help take your line there.

- Practice these with a metronome. It's easy to speed up or slow down rhythmic fills and really, they should be used to help control the energy of the time. When playing skip notes make sure they're serving their intended rhythmic purpose, otherwise they become a detriment by upsetting the pulse.

- When playing in a group, watch the drummer's hands at the end of a phrase—a lot of neat rhythmic hookups can happen at the ends of phrases. By watching a drummer's hands, you can anticipate when they'll make a big hit and join them. Common places for this are the and of beat 4.

- *Don't overdo it!* A line with clear note choice and pulse doesn't need much else to make it sound good.

One more thing to try...

At this point you should have an understanding of how bass lines are harmonically constructed, along with an idea of how rhythmic activity can be added. With this information, go back through the book examples/your own written examples and begin adding eighth notes, triplets, syncopations, and any other rhythmic material that may seem appropriate. Play these with a group. Get feedback from your band mates. Ask them if they notice the music having a different "feel" or "energy." Now that you know how these additions can be placed in your line, your choices will be much more guided and musical.

www.ingramcontent.com/pod-product-compliance
Lightning Source LLC
Chambersburg PA
CBHW062133160426
43191CB00013B/2285